The Scottish Football Book No 23

D1028030

Airdrie's goalkeeper Marshall Poulton
making a gallant save against Clydebank

THE SCOTTISH FOOTBALL BOOK No 23

Edited by Hugh Taylor

Stanley Paul, London

Stanley Paul & Co Ltd
3 Fitzroy Square, London W1

An imprint of the Hutchinson Publishing Group

London Melbourne Sydney Auckland
Wellington Johannesburg and agencies
throughout the world

First published 1977
© Stanley Paul & Co Ltd 1977

Printed in Great Britain by litho at
The Anchor Press Ltd and bound by
Wm Brendon & Son Ltd, both of
Tiptree, Essex

ISBN 0 09 131241 8

Colour photographs of Partick Thistle matches
(page 3 of colour section) by Martin Wright.
All others by Colosport.

CONTENTS

THE EDITOR SAYS...

Once again the big problem in Scottish football is the decline in attendances. Once again, too, many people in soccer blame television for the big drop in gates.

But another reason is that modern football lacks entertainment. The game has become stereotyped and overloaded with tactics. There's a dearth of characters, of artists. Alas, the game isn't likely to change now.

Yet one or two rules could be introduced which would brighten football. For instance, why not ban passing back to the goalkeeper from outside the penalty area? Nothing annoys the fans more – well, except the deliberate use of the offside trap. So why not have lines dotted across the field, with no offside between them? Anything, I say, to bring fresh interest to a game which has lost some of its former glitter.

I believe, too, attention should be paid to Alex Ferguson, that enthusiastic manager who has revived soccer interest in Paisley and made St Mirren a team everyone wants to watch.

The St Mirren Manager insists that the basic football skills which Scotland has always claimed as her heritage are being tragically ignored at the grass roots level of the game. 'We're in danger of producing robot-like players in the future,' he says. And he's got a point.

Alex considers that there's a growing trend in schools and youth football to put

St Mirren Manager Alex Ferguson

the quest for cups and medals before the encouragement of fundamental skills. Too many teachers, he feels, are dabbling with tactics they know little about – instead of simply allowing the boys to enjoy football.

And, in this new *Scottish Football Book*, you can read about a novel idea of former Scotland captain George Young, who also abhors the modern robot-style. His dream? The foundation of a real school for football.

Says Alex Ferguson: 'We must get our priorities right. We hear too many TV pundits talking about things like target men, checking back and laying off. Boys have to realize the joy of playing football before they can truly express themselves on the field but today they're not allowed to. Their heads are being filled with meaningless jargon.

'Let's get back to the basics before it's too late and allow the youngsters to develop their skills and concentrate on things like ball control, balance and kicking a ball.'

How right Alex Ferguson is. Football is becoming a drill. The joy is departing and the sooner more freedom of expression is allowed the players, the quicker the fans will come back.

It was thought the Premier League would bring more competition to Scottish football but already there are grave doubts about that. Are ten clubs too few? Many people say the division should consist of 12 clubs. But Celtic Manager Jock Stein has this to say:

'There is just no room for another two

7

A moment of joy for promoted St Mirren as Bobby Reid scores a goal.

clubs in the league. How would you compile a fixture list? Play each other three times? No League Championship would be genuine if half of the clubs had more home matches than away and vice versa.

'And if, say, we played a team twice on their ground one year and they were relegated would that mean the promoted side having to come to us twice the following year? Hardly fair.

'I still think the increased competition which was the essence of the reconstruction argument has been achieved. Now we have to hope that more attention will be paid to quality. But no matter what anyone says, you can't do without tactics. The world's best teams are all rigidly organized – but they are still brilliant and thrilling to watch. It's the blend that matters.'

For managers, 1976–77 was a sad season, and too many well-known faces departed the soccer scene. Scotland took a blow when manager Willie Ormond resigned to take over Hearts at Tynecastle.

St Mirren goalkeeper Donald Hunter in action

All, however, was not gloom and despondency. What a blow for brighter football was struck by St Mirren, whose enthusiastic and skilful play brought smiles and pride to the old town of Paisley. Gates at Love Street doubled as the Saints marched into the Premier League.

And no praise can be high enough for Clydebank, who were also promoted. Thirteen years ago the Bankies didn't exist. Now they are famous.

It was sad to see a club of the stature of Hearts go down – but they failed sadly. Kilmarnock, too, took the drop but they had the satisfaction of knowing that they went down bravely for they had always tried to play entertaining football.

Football, however, will continue to live, despite the pessimists. It matters too much to this country – and this country will continue to produce some of the greatest players in the world. Let's hope they get the chance to develop naturally.

Hugh Taylor

9

THE WEMBLEY WRECKERS

Scotland's football fans, the vociferous legions whose fervent encouragement makes their team click, tell the world they are the greatest anywhere. Alas, the world has a different view, especially after these thousands of celebrating supporters wrecked Wembley on 4 June 1977.

What a blow these people struck for Scotland – what a dreadful blow! Scotland had played tremendously well to beat an admittedly poor England side 2–1. And then it all happened. . . .

The Scots poured on to the field. They tore down the goalposts. They dug up the turf, smashed seats and caused thousands of pounds worth of damage to the stadium. They became demented, a wild, jubilant, swirling mass of supporters who vaulted barriers and invaded the pitch. Almost every Scot in the stadium – and there were around 70000 – seemed to be out there with the seething, bustling Tartan Army.

It took more than 100 police, some mounted and some on foot, half an hour to clear the ground. Once they had steered the thousands away the whole of the pitch was scarred where the turf had been torn away.

This was the day London belonged to Scotland and where were there ever scenes like these – groups of fans dancing reels in

the middle of the pitch, carrying their flags and finally marching away the post, the bar and the net!

It didn't do Scotland's image much good, however. But the Scots on parade at Wembley during the match did us proud.

Under new Manager Ally MacLeod, Scotland played with distinction, purpose and poise. Nevertheless, England were unbelievably bad, one of the worst Saxon sides to have turned out at Wembley.

Not for ten years had Scotland won at Wembley. Indeed, it had been only two years since England slaughtered us 5–1 in the stadium.

How different this time, how wonderfully different!

Right from the start England struggled to find cohesion and some form of team identity. But Scotland the Great were always the more sophisticated and polished team. It was Scotland who played the football, with Don Masson and Asa Hartford slowing the pace at will and the strength of Bruce Rioch, Scotland's new captain, making the blue midfield supreme.

Above all there was Danny McGrain, Scotland's Player of the Year, showing why he is a world class defender. Whether covering, tackling, jinking forward past embarrassed challengers or releasing the ball long or short with superb effect, the Celt looked what he is – a master at the height of his powers.

More balanced and confident than England, Scotland made virtual tram-lines

What victory to Scotland really means especially when it's England who have been beaten. Scottish fans congratulate Gordon McQueen.

The goal that won the game for Scotland at Wembley. You can hardly see scorer Kenny Dalglish but you can see the ball alright – in the net!

down their right flank to attack Mills, the England back, who had to resort to crude and clumsy fouls at times to stop Kenny Dalglish. And in the 14th minute Scotland should have gone ahead after sustained pressure.

Masson, who had been taking all the Scottish set pieces, flighted a superb free kick into the English goal-mouth and Joe Jordan was allowed to run late and unhindered but was woefully misguided with a header which flew over the bar.

The English defence had been caught in a stupor. Bereft of the dossiers which Don Revie used to prepare on the opposition, they had forgotten Masson's delicate touch and Jordan's massive threat in the air.

Certainly they had forgotten about Gordon McQueen. And how the English rued that fact!

On the brink of half-time Scotland attacked down their left flank. Neal handled just outside the penalty area. A raucous bawl from the clans split the air as Hartford swung the ball into the goal and the long-haired McQueen was there leaping to head the ball past a helpless Ray Clemence. Once again the England defence had been an untidy mess and Scotland justly took the lead.

It had not, however, been a classic first half. Scotland were well ahead but

It was tough at Wembley — and tough indeed for England back Mick Mills who had a trying time against Kenny Dalglish.

Wembley was no place for faint hearts with ferocious tackling by both sides. It was hardly a charming atmosphere. All England seemed to be doing was stifling the match, trying to play it tight and overcome the blatant ineffectiveness of their left flank in which only Kennedy was a genuine left-sided player.

13

Once Scotland had been stirred by McQueen's brilliantly headed goal, however, and the attack had been given a transfusion of energy and variety by the substitution of little Lou Macari for Jordan, who had been injured, the match began to flow relentlessly in Scotland's favour.

England substituted Cherry for Greenhoff and the dashing winger, Tueart, for Kennedy but that had a less decisive influence than Macari's arrival.

So, with Macari bringing a new verve to the attack and Hartford's spirit at last earning the reward of a dominating presence from midfield forward, Scotland asserted themselves convincingly through the first quarter of an hour of the second half.

By the 62nd minute they were two goals ahead.

And what a brilliant goal the second one was – a touch of old Scottish magic, a goal to make the Wembley visit worthwhile.

A cunning, well-timed pass by Hartford inside Neal on the left wing enabled Willie Johnston, who hadn't been much in the match, to show his value on the touchline. Willie swung a long centre from the by-line to Rioch. The captain's header was cheekily flicked on by Macari and although Dalglish's first shot was blocked he persisted stubbornly until the ball was forced into the net.

By the time Archie Gemmill, who had been Scotland's last captain, replaced Masson six minutes from the finish the Scots on and off the field felt secure.

But our nerves suffered the old familiar fraying when England were awarded a penalty with less than three minutes left.

As the Scottish fans were baying: 'Oh, why are we so good?' and tauntingly bawling 'Easy, easy', disaster struck. England had, to their credit, thrown everything into a final flourish.

Alan Rough, who had been so steady, pluckily charged out of goal to cut off a Tueart header. Then the sprinting Trevor Francis fell in the penalty area. To McQueen's surprise the referee pointed to the spot. It didn't look like a foul to the Scots but Mike Channon wasn't worried. He scored neatly and for two minutes there was fear in tartan hearts as England fought valiantly to notch the equalizer. Sweat was lost – but a goal wasn't. And Scotland won a famous victory.

The Scots will never forget Wembley 1977 – neither will the stadium authorities.

For Scotland it was again a match won in the midfield and undoubtedly we have the best players for these positions in Europe today, with a tempting variety offered to team boss Ally MacLeod, who said after the game: 'That was my proudest moment ever.'

The win gave Scotland the home international championship for the second year running – and a tonic on the eve of their arduous trip to South America.

Even the sad Don Revie paid tribute to Ally MacLeod's new Wembley Wizards. He said: 'Scotland played well and I stick to my opinion that they have the best squad in the British Isles.'

The result made up – for the Scots, at least – for many unsavoury moments in the game. Said Hungarian referee Karoly Palotai, who had booked four players: 'It was as tough an international as I have ever refereed. Players spared no effort and tackling was fierce.' But when isn't it in a Scotland–England clash?

Anyhow, all ended well for Scotland – a fine team with a bright future, a good style, one or two players of genius and, in Ally MacLeod, a new manager who has the knack of getting the best out of his players and who wants Scotland to play in the modern manner.

The sad part of Wembley 1977. Scottish fans invade the pitch and destroy the goalposts.

The teams were: England – Clemence (Liverpool), Neal (Liverpool), Watson (Manchester City), Hughes (Liverpool – captain), Mills (Ipswich), B. Greenhoff (Manchester United), Talbot (Ipswich), Kennedy (Liverpool), Francis (Birmingham), Channon (Southampton), Pearson (Manchester United).
Subs: Cherry (Leeds) for Greenhoff, Tueart (Manchester City) for Kennedy.

Scotland – Rough (Partick Thistle), McGrain (Celtic), Forsyth (Rangers), McQueen (Leeds), Donachie (Manchester City), Rioch (Everton – captain), Masson (Queen's Park Rangers), Hartford (Manchester City), Dalglish (Celtic), Jordan (Leeds), Johnston (West Bromwich Albion).
Subs: Macari (Manchester United) for Jordan, Gemmill (Derby) for Masson.
Referee: K. Palotai (Hungary).

THE CHARGE OF THE RED BRIGADE
Aberdeen extra special in League Cup Triumph

One of the biggest football crowds Aberdeen has ever known packed into Pittodrie Stadium on the afternoon of 7 November 1976. Excitement boiled over. Fans wept for joy. Flags, scarves, rosettes and caps formed a brilliant red curtain over the granite city. The cheering might have been heard in Peterhead.

Yet there wasn't even a match being played.

The fans turned out on the Sunday to celebrate the charge of the Red Brigade and Pittodrie became the kingdom of manager Ally MacLeod who, in a year, had taken Aberdeen from an embarrassing position in the Premier League to cup-winners.

For once, though, the energetic, fast-talking football boss was at a loss for words. Like his players, he was overwhelmed by the enthusiastic reception the delirious Aberdonians had accorded the team.

It was the greatest day in Ally's life and it was like the League Cup Final all over again with more than 20000 supporters roaring with delight as the trophy was shown to them by the players.

In Glasgow, however, thousands of Celtic fans walked around in a daze, unable to believe that their team had been beaten by Aberdeen.

And only a few hours before, with the 90 minutes of the League Cup Final nearing an end, there had seemed little possibility of a smile cracking the old grey face of Aberdeen.

The red-clad backs of Aberdeen were firmly against the wall. Celtic were in complete command. It seemed only a matter of time until they scored the winning goal. Wave after wave of green and white lashed the Dons defenders.

Hampden had seldom seen a more dramatic switch.

Not that the crowd of 69707 who had appeared on a dismal day were complaining. For the League Cup Final of 6 November had exploded into one of the best of the series. The teams seemed well matched, despite the vivid contrast in the achievements of the managers. For Celtic's Jock Stein the prize was the twenty-fifth major trophy of his career as a boss. Ally MacLeod was seeking his first.

The first half lived up to expectations. Play was brilliant, with an abundance of fine, thrilling football, exciting challenges and narrow escapes.

Aberdeen had the edge. They weren't overawed by the occasion and played their brand of attractive football. It was Celtic, however, who were first to strike.

In 12 minutes Ken Dalglish broke through on his own. Drew Jarvie brought the Celtic skipper tumbling down and referee John Paterson had no hesitation in awarding a penalty, despite Aberdeen protests. Dalglish picked himself up to ram the ball past Bobby Clark from the spot with all the confidence in the world.

Aberdeen refused to be upset, though play grew bitter. Dalglish and Joe Harper niggled nastily and then Danny McGrain was booked for a foul on Jocky Scott. It was red-blooded all right and Harper became the second player to be cautioned. All the time, though, Aberdeen had been playing with verve and they gained a superb equalizer in the 25th minute. They had been swarming menacingly round Peter Latchford in the Celtic goal and no one looked more likely to bring disaster to the Parkhead club than the sprightly Arthur Graham.

Cutting in swiftly, he swung the ball over to Harper, who passed to Jarvie and from six yards Drew headed into the net – a beautifully made and lethally executed goal. And it was no more than Aberdeen deserved.

The red-bedecked fans in the crowd went wild with delight and Aberdeen stepped up the pace. This goal might have led to others, for the Dons were in charge. Celtic, indeed, had to wait anxiously until the brief period before the interval to threaten the Aberdeen defence on a couple of occasions.

On one of those Danny McGrain sent Paul Wilson streaking down the right. His cross found Johnny Doyle in the clear but the ball broke off the winger's shin and a rare scoring chance was lost.

What a transformation after the interval! After Roy Aitken and Andy Lynch had been cautioned, Celtic settled.

As they turned on that old Parkhead style there was an uneasy silence among the Aberdeen supporters. It was unbelievable that Aberdeen, so clever in the first half, sagged as they did. It was also unbelievable that Celtic failed to score. Jock Stein brought on the veteran Bobby Lennox in place of young Tommy Burns – and that added even more gusto to the Celtic raids.

We've done it! All the joy in the world is on the face of Aberdeen manager Ally MacLeod as he hugs Drew Jarvie at the end of the League Cup Final.

What a grand and glorious feeling to be
winners. Aberdeen players fill the League
Cup with champagne at Hampden.

Bobby Clark became the Dons hero, making one valiant save after another. Aberdeen brought on Davie Robb for the tiring Jarvie. Still Celtic pressed. And Aberdeen had the escape of the final when Wilson hammered a close-range shot against the post.

It was a nightmare for the Dons fans – and for the Celtic supporters.

Clark saved heroically at the feet of Ronny Glavin; Wilson shot wide from ten yards; McGrain missed by inches. So it went on, Aberdeen being sorely battered, Celtic failing to take their glorious chances.

Could the Dons hold out?

One man was never in doubt. He was inspired goalkeeper Bobby Clark. For the veteran had a premonition on the Friday night before the match, and he told team-mate Davie Robb:

'I've dreamed that you'll come on as substitute and score the winning goal. You've been the workhorse of the team for years without receiving any glory – but you'll get it this time.'

Was Clark right?

The first period of extra time had hardly started when confident Celtic were rattled when, like a bolt from the blue, Aberdeen scored.

And it was Robb who notched it, just as Bobby Clark had forecast.

It was hardly a glorious goal – but it was the most important Robb had ever scored. Once again the darting Arthur Graham made a great swerving run across the field. Jocky Scott was in the right position. He crossed and in a mix-up by Celtic defenders and Aberdeen attackers, several of whom missed the ball, Robb stepped in to scramble the ball home at the post.

What a set-back for Celtic! What a kiss of life for Aberdeen! And that goal made

the extra time as exciting as the first half, for Aberdeen came back into sparkling life.

Yet Celtic fought furiously. Glavin almost equalized with a dipping shot, and Clark made a spectacular save from a free kick, also taken by Glavin. At the other end, Aberdeen almost went further ahead when Harper hit a post.

And then it ended, with Aberdeen 2–1 winners of a magnificent League Cup Final.

A sea of red and white swamped the west terracing – and the Aberdeen supporters enjoyed their moment of stupendous triumph.

None more than Bobby Clark, though. Not only did the keeper inspire his colleagues, helping them with his premonition story, but also he played – and played brilliantly – with a broken thumb.

All Celtic took was sympathy. Seldom had they played so well – in the second half – made so many chances, and gained nothing. 'If you don't put the ball in the net, you don't win. That's the sad truth,' said manager Jock Stein afterwards. 'We did enough to win but we didn't. Aberdeen scored and we didn't. There are no excuses from us.' The statistics, though, prove how the game flowed. Astonishingly, Celtic had fifteen corners, Aberdeen only one.

The neutrals were happy. Certainly Aberdeen did a major service for Scottish football when they won the League Cup for the first time in twenty-one years, for they proved that provincial clubs can be winners, and can break through to a top honour without being immediately plundered of their best players. Everyone hoped Aberdeen's success would help encourage other clubs in a similar situation to have a real go.

And manager Ally MacLeod pledged that he would do his utmost to keep his team intact, good news for the Dons fans who remembered that in the past every provincial club who achieved a success had seen the side quickly and systematically broken up by the transfer of key players.

Motherwell and Dundee suffered in the 60s and the fine Aberdeen team of the early 70s, Scottish Cup-winners and twice runners-up to Celtic in the League, lost stars such as Joe Harper (now back) and Martin Buchan.

So it has gone on for years, with the small clubs being condemned to an occasional flash in the pan with no consistent share of the glory.

Let's hope Aberdeen are the exception and that there's a new dawn in Scottish football, with a real challenge to the Old Firm of Rangers and Celtic.

The teams at Hampden were:

Aberdeen: Clark, Kennedy, Williamson, Smith, Garner, Miller, Sullivan, Scott, Harper, Jarvie, Graham. Subs: Robb, Fleming.

Celtic: Latchford, McGrain, Lynch, Edvaldsson, MacDonald, Aitken, Doyle, Glavin, Dalglish, Burns, Wilson. Subs: McClusky, Lennox.

Referee: J. Paterson, Bothwell.

TACTICS—A DIRTY WORD or the Secret of Soccer Success?

As the lights went out in Europe for Scottish club football last season, the howl went up that our players lacked the basic skills, that too many couldn't even control the ball.

Certainly it was a dismal situation for a once-proud football nation – Celtic, Rangers, Hearts and Hibs all out of the major competitions with hardly a blow struck. Certainly our representatives lacked class.

And certainly we see even in the Premier League an appalling number of so-called soccer stars running themselves into the ground and failing to trap, pass and shoot with conviction, all convinced that there is no substitute for sweat.

Critics blamed the emphasis on coaching for the fact that Scotland, who have produced some of the finest and most talented players the world has known, had more willing workhorses than skilful dribblers and passers.

I feel there's some truth in that, for the new breed of football coach distrusts individual brilliance and so the cult of the mediocre has taken over.

But I'm also convinced that we are still far behind in tactics. Tactics? A dirty word to some but certainly more important than many think. Ferenc Puskas, one of the all-time greats, thought so, for he once said:

'The history of war proves that tactics are the most important thing in winning battles. The same thing applies to football matches. Here, too, one must consider the opportunities of both sides and when both sides are of equal strength it is the side with the better tactics that will win.'

What are tactics? Simply, the main aim of tactics is to achieve numerical superiority at the vital place, at the vital time. And you must realize that in football, if it is not the surprise element which brings about success, it is the presence of one more man at the vital moment which will result in a successful tactical manoeuvre.

Talk of tactics, however, brings back the old cry: 'But who would want to watch Continental football . . . it would drive British fans daft . . . Britons want red-hot action and fierce assaults.'

Sometimes I'm not so sure. It would be nice if we could see our teams playing like Real Madrid, the Brazilians or the Hungarians, not aping Inter-Milan. But for the fan of today the main thing – perhaps the only thing – is to support a winning team. The system is set – it puts winners first. The crowds go with success. You may say that if every team were as well organized as Liverpool, the Italians or Bayern Munich you'd have a game of chess and sheer boredom. But if that organized team were winning every week, even if only by a goal, you must admit the terracings would be

Undoubtedly Helenio Herrera of Inter-Milan was a master of tactics, and here you see him telling his players what it's all about in a a talk on strategy on a visit to Scotland.

The right blend of tactics and great natural players – that was the Celtic team of the 1960s, seen here celebrating after beating Hiberian in a League Cup Final.

packed. The supporter today insists on winning – and he isn't too worried about how success is achieved.

I must say I'd love to see a Scottish club succeed again in Europe. To do that, the team must be like the Celtic of Lisbon. It must combine brilliant tactics with a few players of world class.

Remember that when Celtic won the European Cup – and with a team composed entirely of Scotsmen – the tactics set by manager Jock Stein were magnificent, a mixture of the old and the new, with an accent on attack which baffled the cautious Inter-Milan. Remember that Celtic had at least three players of world stature, Murdoch, Johnstone and Auld.

Today two schools of thought rule in football. Still on top are those who favour safety-first tactics, having their teams rely on defence with the odd brisk surprise counter-attack. This attitude is summed up by the famous (or, to some, notorious) formula of the Arsenal manager Herbert Chapman, who said: 'If you don't have a goal scored against you, one point is in the kitty. If you manage to score a goal yourself, all two points are yours.'

The other – and more modern – school favours positive or what is now known as total football. Only a few, however, feel attack should take precedence over defence, though they think soccer is about scoring more goals than the opposing side.

Frankly, defence rules in top-class football. Attacks by the best teams of today start from defence. And the number one rule in modern football is: you must have an organized defence.

My prayer for Scottish football is that we discover a genius who can come up with a new idea. After all, it was Scotland who brought in the first tactics. Queen's Park introduced the passing game, as opposed to the ideas of the teams of the time of scrambling the ball in pell-mell rushes into the goal. Queen's put the emphasis on teamwork, playing a superior, more open brand of football.

This necessitated the use of the whole pitch and, to accommodate this innovation, depth throughout the team was essential. So the formation of two backs, two half-backs and six forwards was adopted. Later this became the 2–3–5 formation – a style so many people still say would make football more attractive.

You'll notice 'depth' was the operative word when Queen's started to play more scientific soccer. It still is today, for not so long ago, when we lost in Prague to Czechoslovakia, former Scotland manager Willie

Ormond was moaning that because Eddie Gray, that fine left winger, was absent, our team lacked the necessary 'depth'. For depth read space. And there you have the basis of tactics – the team who makes best use of the open spaces wins most times.

Since the old Queen's Park days we have had many formations and today it seems that the magic figures are 4–4–2. Alas, all changes have been made in one direction – from attack to defence. Originally, teams had nine forwards and one defender but gradually the number of all-out attackers has been reduced and the number of full-time defenders increased. The aim is now to concede fewer goals than your opponents. Originally, it was to score more goals than your rivals.

What I'd like to see today are more positive tactics. Once again Celtic are showing the way in Scotland with a style that is scientific but also intriguing to watch – scientific and based on attack.

My old friend Danny Blanchflower, that great Irish player and manager whose sole aim is to provide flowing, skilful football, sums it up best.

He told me not so long ago:

'What we need in British football today is a change of attitude. Tactics are important – but are we providing the right tactics?

'There are too many managers and too many coaches who tell players what they must *not* do and too few who really give their players positive instructions.

'We must get the right British style. After all, overseas teams still fear our pace and stamina. If we could get more skill, more ideas into our play and weld these to our natural game we could still be the best in the world.'

Danny likes football to be free and flowing – but he is also a tactical genius, as he showed when he played for Spurs. And this bold Irishman claims that one aspect of modern tactics was introduced by Northern

Ireland – the practice of lining up defensive walls at free kicks. Grins Danny:

'It happened because we had a goalkeeper who couldn't see 30 yards. So instead of having forwards who stood on the half-way line wondering whether a free kick would bring a goal or not, we brought them back to form a wall.

'I took the idea back to Tottenham and it spread from there.'

What must be drummed into our teams today is the fact that players must remember that no matter where a side has possession of the ball that said side should consider themselves in an attacking phase – as most good teams of the modern era start their attacking football from the back. This calls for hard work and good unselfish off-ball running by every defender as well as forwards – and it also calls for imagination.

In attack, it is essential that the whole forward line is capable of working to the limit in producing mobility with the final effect of an unorthodox approach.

The main theme in attacking football is producing situations whereby you are placing two forwards against a defender, commonly known as 'two against one' or 'three against two'.

These situations call all the time for intelligent reading of the game and the necessary will to work hard. Too many players fail to appreciate that it is easier to beat one with two and, because of lack of effort, fail to make themselves the extra man, having a tendency to stand and watch. Most successful attacking moves are based on the factor of forwards running intelligently, either in position to take part, or in positions solely to act as decoys to disguise the final thrust on goal.

What I'd like to see in Scotland is a team playing a combination of the tactics of Real Madrid and the Hungarians – the best football teams I have ever watched. A dream? Perhaps. But some day a genius might find the right players and pick the most fascinating facets of the styles of these sides and put Scotland back on top of the world.

Just how did these famous elevens play? The Hungarians were more tactically aware than Real, who had so many artistic players that they didn't have to put the same emphasis on tactics as lesser clubs.

The tactic which made the Hungarians of the 1950s great was a change in the formation of their forward line in an attempt to disorganize defences used to the W-M formation, which involved turning the centre-half (who used to be an attacking player) into a third back.

The Hungarians made their inside-forwards play well upfield, withdrawing the centre-forward and the two wingers. An attacking wing-half linked up with the centre-forward in midfield, while the other wing-half concentrated on defence. The defence was solid but hardly as brilliant as that of the Swiss or the Italians of a later era. But the Hungarian forwards were magnificent – and would probably have been successful under any formation. Nevertheless, their M attack contributed to their early success.

Teams meeting the Hungarians were uncertain. The centre-back wouldn't know whether to follow the deep-lying centre-forward and be drawn out of position or remain in the middle with two inside-forwards to face.

The full-backs would be uneasy about marking deep-lying wingers. If they marked the wingers closely they would leave big gaps behind them. Wing-halves were faced with the problem of marking two extremely dangerous inside-forwards who remained upfield. If they did decide to mark the inside-forwards the whole team suffered because the wing-halves were responsible with their inside-forward colleagues for the scheming of the whole team and thus they blew up.

The obvious way to counteract the M

forward line was to revert to the attacking centre-half formation in defence, using man-to-man marking. Yes, tactics do matter. For the Germans, having been defeated by the Hungarians in the early stage of World Cup 1954, produced just that defensive system in the final – and shocked the arro-

Many Scots say to hell with tactics – give us players with real flair. This, they say, is what football is all about – a tricky player (in this case Bobby McKean of Rangers) slips neatly round a defender.

gant Hungarians, the top team in the world then, by winning 3–2.

27

Nevertheless, the Hungarians of that era were extremely skilful and adept at ball-holding and close, quick interpassing. As with many teams of today, the Hungarians played much of their football in their own half. For this enticed the opposing defence to move forward, thus leaving behind them large open spaces which were utilized by quick-thinking forwards.

And this is something our teams in Europe should think about before they say they'll rely on British power and speed to wear down the Continental defences. How often does it happen? Seldom! But how often are our teams, on the attack, suddenly outwitted by a cunning thrust by a European team? All too often!

The Hungarians used a particular formation to suit their players. But Real Madrid developed tactics and formations to suit new inclusions in their team. They had the pick of the top players in the world and produced some of the best football ever seen. Real players were so good, so versatile, that they could alter their tactics from game to game.

Can you, then, imagine a team using the tactics of the Hungarians and the talents of Real? That team would rule the world.

And this all goes to prove that style alone, tactics alone, great players alone are not the answer to soccer success. All have a vital role to play. It's the blend that really matters.

THE BEST BACK IN THE WORLD
Danny McGrain is Everyone's Player of the Year

It is not of full-backs that the Scottish troubadours sing and heroic tales are told. The legends have usually been woven around dashing centre-forwards, suave wingers or masters of the inside-forward craft.

True, now and again we read headlines which talk about 'Princely Pairs of the Past' and we sigh as we think about notable full-back partnerships like Young and Cox of Rangers, Kilmarnock and Shaw of Motherwell (who played 341 Scottish League and Cup games together), Alex Hamilton and Bobby Cox of Dundee, Dougie Sharpe and Jimmy Binning of Queen of the South, Murphy and Haddock of Clyde, Robertson and Nibloe of Kilmarnock, McNair and Dodds of Celtic.

Alas, we seldom consider these mighty men as artists. We think of them as players bred to determination and destruction, men with hearts of oak and limbs of steel, who punted the ball mightily and were not averse to banging diminutive wingers over the touchline and on to the track.

In the old days the job of the back was to stop movements by attackers. That was all. His quality was judged by his pre-eminence in long kicking. As a boy, I gazed enraptured at the balls cleared by the massive legs of Kilmarnock's Joe Nibloe at Rugby Park. The football soared in majestic high arcs into the clear blue Ayrshire sky, for Joe could leather it from one end of the Rugby Park pitch to the other.

From the back of yesterday was expected husky tackling, grimness, anger and dis-putation. Only the physical was looked for; the cerebral was out, wasn't even wanted.

The daddy of all the great backs of yesteryear was the doughty Walter Arnott of Queen's Park, who played for Scotland against England ten times last century.

'A giant among giants' was how the formidable Walter was described. 'When he made a sudden rush at an opponent, he moved like a whirlwind.'

Arnott was the model for backs. Safety first was the motto. Subtlety was frowned on. And that was why few backs ever became the subjects of autobiographies, cigarette cards or startling transfers. Why, some people didn't even think full-backs were footballers at all.

Now, however, with changes in soccer style, the role of the back is more complex and the modern defender of eminence is built more constructively and not only stops but starts action. Now full-blooded kicking (of ball and winger) is a mark of poor workmanship. Now the back wins fame by manoeuvre and attacking ability. And the standard set by such as Jimmy Carabine of Third Lanark and Andy Beattie of Preston North End has been surpassed by many backs, now as talented, as artistic and as invaluable to a team as a scheming inside-forward.

Moment of triumph for Danny McGrain, Scotland's Player of the Year. Scotland have just beaten England and, with Celtic team-mate Kenny Dalglish, Danny takes a firm grip of the British championship trophy at Hampden.

And there is little doubt that everyone's player of the year is a full-back – Danny McGrain of Celtic. Many of his colleagues declare that he is the best full-back not only in Scotland or Europe but in the world.

The McGrain style is vastly different from that of the player who bore that accolade before him – George Young. Big George was the master of defence. Danny

Danny McGrain is not only a defender. He is one of the most feared attacking backs in Europe. And here he takes on the Aberdeen rearguard in a vigorous raid.

McGrain is the master of total football, of manoeuvre. Young was as imperturbable as Ailsa Craig, with reassuring bulk. McGrain crackles into attack and he is fast, slick, elusive as well as a powerful tackler and brilliant reader of the defensive game.

Young stood out as a Colossus and he was the key man in the Rangers strategy of the 1950s. That involved defenders using a powerful punt into the opposition goal area, which allowed the Ibrox forwards to score goals in a smash-and-grab fashion.

Some critics had no liking for the area of 50 yards divided by the midfield line be-

coming a soccer Sahara, saying football had become too streamlined and deprived of beauty because of the disappearance of skilful approach work, the happy cohesion between wing-halves and inside-forwards, the sudden burst down the line by wingers.

But there was beauty in the skill and accuracy of Young's lobs. And it is more difficult to kick the ball accurately a distance of 60 yards than to pass it 10 yards.

McGrain, however, is more than a defender. Young never pretended to be anything except a reassuring back or centre-half. In today's more fluent concept McGrain plays a vital role. He is the complete footballer. He is also one of the few footballers who satisfies on a double count: great skill, big heart. No one gives more pleasure to the enthusiast than Danny McGrain. Indeed, there would be headlines if Danny ever played a bad game.

Off the field, Danny is a quiet lad – solid, efficient, dependable, abhorring publicity. Kilmarnock manager Willie Fernie, who coached McGrain in his early years at Parkhead, sums up the Scotland defender best. Says Willie:

'One of the many things Charlie Tully used to tell me was: "You have 110 yards by 70 every Saturday to say all you have to say about football." That's Danny McGrain. He says it all on the park.'

On the transfer market McGrain must be worth £500000. He is the man most fitted to play a key role in the modern formation, which is known as the Whirl, a style of football evolved by Dr Willy Meisl, one of the great thinkers. In this pattern the emphasis is speed of thought rather than speed of the ball. And no one thinks faster than Danny McGrain. Quick thinking is the way to success in today's total football.

Danny is modest, though. He says: 'If you're a player with a big club you're there to be built up one day and knocked down the next so it's best to say nothing and just get on with the job.'

McGrain considers his first priority is to defend, even though he is best known for his attacking prowess. He says:

'My main job is to prevent goals but obviously I do like to link up with the attack when I can. Anyhow, how successful a player is, is largely dependent on how good a side he is in and I have been lucky over the years at Parkhead, playing with some outstanding colleagues.

'I prefer playing against orthodox wingers because that way you know where you are.'

Danny McGrain's greatest admirers are among the Anglos in the Scotland pool. Tommy Craig of Newcastle United, one of the most artistic players in football, says simply:

'Danny must be the greatest back in the world. He's got everything – intelligence, skill, strength. Perhaps there has never been a better back.'

Sir Alf Ramsey, former England team manager, is another who has been impressed by McGrain. No wonder. There is something of Ramsey in McGrain. And although Sir Alf was never a hero to Scots he was a brilliant back in his day. Never as good in the tackle as McGrain, Ramsey was nevertheless a calm, unhurried, connoisseur's footballer; in defence, that is. McGrain also possesses these qualities which you'll notice if you make a study of the back who has everything.

McGrain's exciting forays are apt to disguise his sterling defensive play.

In the full-backs' Valhalla I'm sure the old-timers, who felt they were never appreciated, must be smiling proudly every time they gaze down on Danny McGrain, the man who has turned the defender's rugged task into a thing of artistry and excitement.

THE PRINCE OF GOALKEEPERS

His friends looked at him, amazed. 'Old Jerry's gone round the bend,' they told each other. And there was ribald comment indeed on the Scottish coalfield away back in 1929. For there was Jerry Dawson spending every lunchtime break kicking lumps of coal about.

The youngster wore out a few pairs of boots but there was method in his madness. His ambition was to become a professional footballer and play for Rangers. And he was good, but, according to Rangers manager Bill Struth, just not good enough, mainly because he couldn't kick a dead ball properly at goal kicks.

The determined Jerry was sure he could conquer that failing and so he practised for weeks hammering away at the lumps of coal. He achieved his ambition. Not only did Jerry become the Rangers keeper but also his name is forever written bold in Scotland's soccer hall of fame as probably the most polished, most graceful, most inspiring goalkeeper Scotland has produced.

Jerry, who died in January 1977, at the age of sixty-seven, was not only a prince of goalkeepers, however. He was a prince of good fellows, a wit, the ideal companion, a man among men.

Asked if his practice on the coalfield helped him, he used to laugh and say: 'Hardly. I was one of the worst goal-kickers

Jerry Dawson, prince of goalkeepers, gives a tip to a goalkeeper of today, Peter McCloy of Rangers.

in Scottish football. I used to fall sideways when I kicked a dead ball and I'm sure that must have given my colleagues at Ibrox many a heart attack.'

What Jerry Dawson didn't say was that his prowess and agility, his sure clutch and his astonishing reflexes put him in the class of the greats and that any club in the world would have been glad of his services and allowed backs to take goal kicks as Rangers so often did.

With the exception of Celtic's John Thomson, who died so young and tragically, no goalkeeper quite caught the public imagination as Dawson did. He joined Rangers in 1929 from Camelon Juniors. His career at Ibrox spanned two decades. He was a hero with Rangers and Scotland, later became manager of East Fife after a spell as keeper with Falkirk, and ended his sporting career in newspapers and publicity.

Jerry was known to thousands long after his football days finished. He was the cheery compère of quiz shows and panel games and he raised countless thousands of pounds for charity through personal appearances for any cause and for any religious denomination.

In his career with Rangers – he played 505 matches for them, 14 for Scotland and won two Scottish Cup medals – there were moments of drama, moments of fun – and moments of terror.

Jerry recalled the infamous Ibrox bottle party of 1941, which, he declared, was as

Great players were with East Fife when Jerry Dawson was manager. Here you see manager Dawson re-signing that brilliant forward Charlie 'Cannon-ball' Fleming.

bad as any war. This is what he said in his own inimitable way:

'As so often happens when you are trying your darndest to avoid trouble, that's when you run into it. And what might be a trivial thing in an ordinary club game can build up suddenly into a major incident when Rangers and Celtic are playing each other.

'A classic example was that Ibrox bottle party on 6 September 1941, when we beat Celtic 3–0 in a Southern League game.

'Aye, it was in the middle of the war but you know Rangers and Celtic fanatics – the war with the Germans was only a side issue for them.

'Anyhow, Celtic were putting us through the mill and had forced several corners. At these corners, Jimmy Delaney was taking up position on my goal-line, standing practically on my toes, and I protested to the referee.

'Rightly, he told me to get on with the game as there was nothing he could do about it. And it was a legitimate tactic as long as Jimmy didn't obstruct me while I was going for the ball.

'Eventually, an in-swinger came across, making for under the bar. With Jimmy tight against me, I jostled him and managed to knuckle the ball clear.

'Delaney lay on the goal-line and there was the referee dramatically pointing to the penalty spot. And it was happening at the end favoured by the Parkhead faithful. The howl of glee as I protested in vain made the Hampden Roar sound like a whisper.

'Then there was the usual big-match hush as a penalty is about to be taken. But the ball was fired near enough to enable me to beat it out.

'And then it all began to happen in a big way. Quicker than any thunderstorm, it rained hundreds of empty bottles. Despite the distance of the terracing from the field, many of the bottles bounced menacingly on the pitch and the game was stopped.

'There, among several other Celtic and Rangers players sheltering in the net, Jimmy Delaney and I stood side by side. We looked on ruefully as reinforcements of police staged a spectacular baton charge to quell the outbreak we had unwittingly sparked off.

'Said Jimmy: "I'll keep well away from you in future, Jerry." And I told him: "I'll be keeping out of your road, too, Jimmy."

'It's the knowledge that you are surrounded by this simmering volcano that is liable to erupt at any time that makes playing in an Old Firm game such a tingling experience.'

In those days Jerry was known as the penalty-kick king – not at taking them but at stopping them – as he did that kick of Celtic's Frank Murphy at the infamous bottle party. What was his secret?

Perhaps it was his gaze. Opposing players were warned that when taking a penalty they should never look at Dawson, for he had a penetrating stare which could almost mesmerize the penalty-taker.

Here's a story from the famous Celtic wing-half George Paterson – a story which shows penalties and bottles figured far too often in Old Firm games of the past.

Said George: 'I remember a crowd of 90000 at an Old Firm clash at Ibrox in 1935. We got a penalty against Rangers and, as our boss, Willie Maley, had a theory that the most inexperienced player in the side should take it, I stepped up – and scored.

Liverpools' former manager Bill Shankly, another of the Scottish football greats, played often with Jerry Dawson for his country, and said Dawson was one of the greatest keepers of all time.

'But the referee ordered a retake because a bottle had been thrown. As the situation was being sorted out, Jerry ambled over to me and said: "Don't bother about taking it again, son. I know exactly where you are going to put it." The Celtic fans were furious. They thought Jerry was having a go at me. But you couldn't take offence at Jerry. Anyhow, I scored the second time.

'But I didn't always meet with that success against Jerry. In a Charity Cup final at Hampden we were awarded three penalties against Rangers. We missed the lot. I took the first and hit the post, Malcolm MacDonald hit the second and drove the

37

This was Jerry Dawson in his heyday with Rangers in the 1930s. Jerry's at the start (left to right) of the back row in a famous group of the Ibrox club which includes Alan Morton, Tommy Muirhead, David Meikeljohn, Bob McPhail, Sandy Archibald, Jimmy Simpson, Jimmy Fleming and George Brown. Ask grandad to pick out his favourite players.

ball past, and Jerry stopped the third which I took.

'I've never seen a grin as wide on anyone's face.'

That was Jerry Dawson – man of many parts, superb keeper and one of life's cheery chappies who kept everyone in his vicinity happy.

Jerry was also one of football's thinkers. And what he had to say away back in 1954 when he was East Fife manager and the British were becoming aware that the threat from the Continent was fast making our game out-of-date, should be seriously considered today when this country is struggling against the top national sides.

The great advantage of foreign teams, Jerry pointed out all those years ago, was that they *put* the ball in the net – they don't *shoot* into the net. That's true.

Watch the Continentals in action and you often feel the goalkeepers aren't up to the standard of the outfield players. But the former Scotland and Rangers keeper had a keen and experienced eye for what was happening. As he said at the time, how many shots in the games between top European sides are net-busters? Precious few.

'That,' he once told me, 'is what Scottish attackers should be copying from the Continentals – their finishing thrust.

'The Continentals build their moves up more patiently than we do and then one nippy forward flashes through to put – not shoot – the ball into the net.

'If the ball is well out of the keeper's reach it is just as impossible for him to save it as it would be if it was the type of shot he couldn't see.

'After all, our most successful and expert penalty kickers aren't the boys who blaze away. They're the lads who place the ball quietly but efficiently well out of the goalie's reach.'

And expounding on his theory of how to score without shooting, Jerry added: 'Almost any Scottish player can pass the ball right to the foot of his team-mate from a range of 10 to 15 yards. No bother at all. He knows exactly how to hit the ball so it will go exactly where he wants it.

'But put the same player 12 to 15 yards from goal with the ball at his feet and what does he do with it? Well, anyone who has spent hours on the terracing can answer that. He'll shoot and the shot will have the muzzle velocity of an anti-tank gun if the player can get his foot properly to the ball.

'About one shot in ten is anywhere near the goal.

'But if the player had felt he was *passing* the ball, right into the empty space between the goalie and a post, he would have had more chance of finding the net.

'I know. I often congratulated forwards of yesteryear on spectacular goals and received the answer: "Och, it was nothing. Ah just put my heid doon and hit it."

'So – to aim is the aim. Hit or miss isn't good enough.'

And that was sound advice. How I wish more of our players would take it nowadays.

Let the great Bill Shankly sum up Dawson, who played in nine wartime internationals: 'I played in the same team as Jerry seven times between 1939 and 1943. Never mind about the war in Europe – this was the war in Glasgow. Scotland played England twice a year in those days and we hadn't too much success. But at the end of it all I had no doubt that Jerry Dawson ranked among the greatest keepers of all time.

'Great players could play in any era. Jerry Dawson would have been just as big a name in today's football.'

As Shankly said, football is a great game and it was people like Jerry Dawson who made it great.

CONTROVERSY–it's the Life Blood of Football

Controversy is the life-blood of football. No one loves to argue more fiercely than the soccer fan.

It's not the major issues of the day that cause the rows. Little things really mean a lot in football. And you've all seen your friends go almost berserk when they claim it was never a penalty, that the striker was offside, that it was a blatant foul.

Every one of us has his pet hate, his pet cause, and how I wish Scottish football would take up a new and good idea – having a kick-in instead of a throw-in.

This suggestion has been the basis of an experiment abroad and several Scottish clubs, including Kilmarnock, are using it in practice games. 'It really works,' says Kilmarnock manager Willie Fernie, 'because it speeds up the game.'

I hope this becomes official soon – and all because I really hate it . . .

. . . when goalkeepers waste time by placing the ball for a goal kick with the utmost care, moving back at a leisurely pace, then changing their mind and beckoning another defender to take the kick . . .

. . . when, at a throw-in, the time-wasting player pretends to take the shy, then hands the ball to a colleague, who steals several yards before being ordered by the referee to go back to the place where the ball was put out of play . . .

. . . when, at a corner kick, a player takes the ball under his arm, toddles towards the corner flag and takes minutes to place the ball.

You'll have gathered I hate time-wasting. I do and I suggest this is something which needs more attention from referees nowadays.

Due to the irritating practice of time-wasting, a match seldom consists of twice 45 minutes of actual play, but of around 30 to 35 minutes each way.

So the paying customer is being cheated.

If referees resorted more energetically to the imposing of the penalties provided, the number of idle runs, the 'empty time' within both portions of 45 minutes, would cease dramatically and games would become more interesting, livelier and much more exciting.

Football, I fear, is in danger of becoming too 'professional' and most fans don't really like anything that savours of sharp practice.

I'd hate it more, though, if we reached the stage of a club in Italy where the underhand is too often relished and the soccer con men are kings – they even had the ball-boys involved falling over the ball and kicking it away for yards when their team was ahead and hanging on for the whistle.

Full-time referees?

This brings me to another controversy. Should referees become full-time? It's not a new idea, but, with football now involving more and more money, becoming more business-like and involving huge rewards, is there really room for semi-pros?

Most referees are against becoming full-time professionals, and there are many objections. It couldn't be done in a season. It would take years. It could also increase the risk of corruption of officials whose livings were totally involved in the game.

Nevertheless, many influential people in football are now convinced that making referees full-time pros is necessary because of a sound thesis: the fact that too many referees are engaged in day-to-day jobs which never involve making vital decisions.

Yet suddenly on a Saturday they are in charge of a business worth millions. Don't forget that the referee is not merely in charge of 90 minutes of football – he is in charge of everyone involved, players, managers, fans and police included.

And it's said that full-time referees would be fitter and thus be better equipped physically to control matches.

The wages, of course, would have to be similar to that of the players – and who'd pay them? By League levy, by some kind of football lottery? And how could a referee, with at most two matches a week, fill in his time? By more training, by teaching up-and-coming whistlers?

I'm afraid that, no matter how desirable the idea, the chance of referees in Scotland becoming full-time is as remote as the chance of winning a Wembley ticket in the public ballot.

Full-time players?

Indeed, the trouble with Scottish football is that too few clubs today are full-time. They just can't afford it. It should make us realize that we are a small country – and blessed with players of such rare inbred talent that we can face up bravely, if not always successfully, to the representatives of bigger and wealthier countries, where football is full-time.

There is too much moaning at the bar about Scottish football. We just will not face reality. Every club wants to be as good and as successful as Rangers or Celtic. How can they be – as part-timers? It's just not on. Football nowadays is big business and you can't succeed as semi-pros.

It's all very well to say soccer is an easy game, but not everyone can play, and the more time players have to perfect their skills and fit into the team blend obviously the better they must be. It's as simple as that.

And until all our clubs are full-time – which will never happen – there's no use moaning about the state of Scottish football.

New rules?

Among the many arguments are those which suggest – like kick-ins for throw-ins – that it's time for some of the rules to be altered. Well, we can't deny that football is still imperfect and there are some changes which might improve it. But you must not interfere with the heart of the game, which beats as strongly as ever. In fact, due mainly to television, there's far too much razzamatazz now, an exaggeration of the trivia and a blurring of the essentials.

Football is more than a glorious goal, a fantastic dribble, a marvellous save. Football is a game of 90 minutes, with hard work, great heart, solid determination – seldom seen on the small screens – being as essential to the build-up of goals as the goals themselves.

Television gives you the golden moments – but television is usually merely a capsule of the great game. It caters for the lazy, the alleged fan who yawns when shots go past or a gruelling battle develops in midfield and who wants only to see an explosive goal.

Who'd be a referee? Certainly they should receive much more money than they do for their tough job, illustrated here by referee John Gordon breaking up trouble in a match between Celtic and Aberdeen.

Look out for new ideas emanating from America, where soccer is starting to sizzle. But let's beware of them. After all, the Americans in all their sports demand prolific scores and, as in basketball, they seek results like 10–9 or even 30–26.

That's why one of their bright suggestions is that the goal be enlarged from its present eight yards wide by eight yards high. The reason? Because the Yanks say goalkeepers have grown bigger over the last hundred years and therefore it is unreasonable to think the goal should have been kept at the same size.

This time John doesn't heed an appeal by former Motherwell star Bobby Watson as he bends over an injured player. Full-time refs? Perhaps it's not a bad idea when you realize what the poor old ref has to put up with in modern soccer.

Is that so? I didn't think the late Jimmy Brownlie was small. He was, I'm told, a colossus. Anyhow, not so long ago, wee Jocky Robertson of Third Lanark was reckoned one of the greatest keepers of all time.

And Jocky was hardly a giant.

Still, its everyone's right to argue about football, if he – or she – is really interested in the beloved game. We should all, however, be sure of our facts before we shout.

For instance, there's a demand that tackling from behind should be banned in Scotland – as, say those in favour, it is in England.

Ah, but they're wrong. Tackling from behind is not banned in England. How can it be? Tackling from behind is not illegal. There's nothing in the laws to make it so.

What happened in England was a campaign begun to ban *foul* tackles from behind, just as foul tackles from the front or the side can be illegal.

It's how it's done that matters. Referees must be wary of this one. A tackle from behind is judged to be legal if the tackler makes contact with the ball first. If he hits his opponent first, it's a foul.

And don't forget that the International Board say in one of their decisions that if a player deliberately turns his back to an opponent when he is about to be tackled he may be charged – but not in a dangerous manner.

Mind you, if I had one wish for football, it would be that our players take lessons from the Continentals in the art of taking penalty-kicks.

For our failure rate in the big competitions from the spot has become so high that it can no longer be put down to coincidence.

I don't think one Scottish club has lived through a sudden-death finish since the penalty ruling was introduced in season 1970–1.

Aberdeen were first to fail that season when Jim Forrest missed a penalty and allowed Honved to win their Cup-winners' Cup-tie by five penalties to four.

The following season Rangers lost a penalty tie-breaker to Sporting Lisbon, though they were later allowed to proceed in the Cup-winners' Cup when it was established that no penalties should have been taken.

In the same season Celtic's European Cup challenge ended when Dixie Deans missed a penalty against Inter-Milan and Celtic lost also on penalties in a match with Benfica.

Failure to score from the spot cost Hibs dearly in their tie with Leeds United in the UEFA Cup. And the less we say about Scotland's record with penalties the better.

Why aren't our modern marksmen deadly? We recall the accuracy of Johnny Hubbard, the venom of Tommy Gemmell; and not so long ago wee Tommy McLenan, when with Kilmarnock, seldom failed.

Listen to Rangers' manager Jock Wallace who says: 'I don't think forwards are the right men to take penalties. Defenders are more used to kicking dead balls. Indeed, in practice, our best penalty kicker is goalkeeper Peter McCloy.'

Yet I sigh when I think how expert are the Continentals.

Mightn't it be a good idea to bring someone over from Europe to show our lads just how it should be done?

OK, OK . . . it's just something else to argue about. . . .

THINGS AIN'T WHAT THEY SEEM TO BE

They certainly aren't — even in football!

For instance, what do you make of this picture? You'd think it was a happy holiday snap of Rangers manager Jock Wallace having a great time on the beach of some paradise isle.

Aye, you'd imagine there's big Jock, full of the joys, at peace with the world, all set for a leisurely swim.

You'd be wrong. And you should just hear what his players are saying about their boss. . . .

What they're really saying – muttered here by Johnny Hamilton – is: 'That big Wallace should be in charge of a concentration camp.

For these are pictures of Hamilton leading his mates up Torture Trail.

Yes, Rangers are on the dreaded sands of Gullane. There, at the start of the season, they sweat and are urged to the limit of their endurance in a training session on the dunes – a training session as tough as anyone could imagine, a session which evokes pictures of the French Foreign Legion in the desert.

Tough? It still makes me shudder to think of Sandy Jardine and his mates going all out up that trail on the dunes. It's heart-breaking, sinew-straining, muscle-sapping work.

It's football's toughest Commando training.

Yet there are smiles from the players at the end, happy cracks with manager Wallace – for the players realize that they have done it . . . gone with flying colours through a test which would upset the world's fittest athletes.

THE GRAY CAVALIER—Andy leaps to Stardom

Young Scot Andy Gray made history in 1977 when he became not only the Footballer of the Year in England but the Young Player of the Year. He was chosen by the men who know best – his fellow professionals south of the border.

What's Andy like? He's one of the nicest, quietest lads in the game – but he will almost certainly become one of the greatest soccer exports from Scotland.

Who discovered him? Dundee United manager Jim McLean was his first boss, after the lad had been spotted by United scout, Maurice Friel.

Here is the Andy Gray story – plus a striking article by manager Jim McLean about how it feels to lose a player he realizes will turn into a glowing star.

You don't call them centre-forwards any more. They're strikers or target men.

And they may have the most difficult task in football. In these days of ruthless defence there's little chance of a striker going through on his own with a glorious dribble or flash of spell-binding speed to finish with a thundering shot. Defences are too tough, too well drilled to allow a glimpse of a Hughie Gallacher or a Jimmy McGrory or Willie Thornton from any attack leader (if you'll pardon the old-fashioned expression).

The striker of today fights a fierce, remorseless battle with his opponents. A battle of brawn. A battle of attrition. A battle to see who'll falter first.

Often the striker has a partner because it has been found that in this foot-to-foot fighting, attack pays off better if more power is pitted against defenders. Often the striker is the man who makes the goals, not the man who scores them, because the weight of his aggression allows a colleague to nip in and whip the ball into the net.

Yet while this may not sound the glamorous position it did in the old days when centre-forwards were dashing cavaliers, the heroes of the fans, the players it was the dream of every schoolboy to emulate, the lads who were given the best chance to show the basic skills of the game – dribbling, shooting, heading, *scoring* – while this may look like the position more suited to an all-in wrestler than a crack footballer, it also has its share of super-stars.

And there is no more exciting striker in Britain than Andy Gray, the young man who went to Aston Villa from Dundee United and now receives all the adulation once reserved for those glamorous adventurers of yesteryear who went south – Alex James, Alex Jackson, Hughie Gallacher.

In the opinion of many managers, English as well as Scottish, Gray is the best centre-forward in British football.

Certainly he is the pin-up boy of Birmingham, his superb goals having brought excitement and hope back to the famous old Villa club.

How, in a position which calls for courage far beyond the call of duty, strength more than skill, has Andy Gray developed into such a glamorous figure?

Opposite: Scotland's captain Bruce Rioch beats off an English challenge during Scotland's Wembley victory.

Hibs' goalkeeper, Mike McDonald misses this one completely as Thistle's Jim Melrose heads for goal at Firhill.

More Firhill thrills — here Celtic goalkeeper Peter Latchford is in trouble as he goes for a ball with Alan Hansen, (now with Liverpool) in the foreground.

Opposite: Two centre-halves in conflict during the Scottish Cup Final — Colin Jackson of Rangers and Roddy McDonald of Celtic get ready to challenge for a ball in this Hampden scene.

Scotland striker, Joe Jordan, rises above the massed English defence at Wembley to reach this ball watched by his club mate from Leeds United, Gordon McQueen.

Willie Donachie in great action against Wales in the Home International Championship.

Celtic and Scotland star Kenny Dalglish fights his way past a determined challenge by Wales' Brian Flynn during the Wrexham International.

Rangers' Tom Forsyth in confident form here for Scotland.

Alan Rough, the Scotland and Partick Thistle goalkeeper is at full stretch here to thwart a Welsh attack in the 0-0 draw last season.

The so-immaculate Don Masson of Queen's Park Rangers sends away a long pass for Scotland watched by team-mate Archie Gemmill.

Opposite top: Alan Rough finishes off that Wrexham save and leaves the Welsh forwards frustrated.

Opposite bottom: Wing play comes back to Wembley! Here is West Brom and Scotland star Willie Johnston baffling England's Phil Neal and Brian Talbot during the Wembley win.

Another scene from Wembley and it's the world's finest right-back, Danny McGrain, going forward into attack for Scotland.

A moment of relaxation for Scotland's Big Two — the Old Firm bosses, Jock Wallace of Rangers and Jock Stein of Celtic.

Because he has native Scottish skill. Because he has found a technique to upset the most flexible defenders. Because he allies a magnificent aerial technique to a sturdy frame able to absorb punishment. And because no striker in the land pounces more venomously on mistakes made by defences.

Let Bobby Robson of Ipswich Town, probably the outstanding manager in England, talk about the young centre-forward who will undoubtedly become as popular with Scottish fans as Lawrie Reilly. The Ipswich manager's admiration for the athletic, good-looking Gray – who stalks the penalty area like a highwayman ready to stage a slick hold-up – sprang from the Scot's performance not so long ago against his team, regarded as the best-organized side south of the border.

'Villa beat us 5–2,' said Robson. 'And it all happened to us and for Gray in the last 30 minutes. We made three mistakes and he punished us unmercifully. I have been in professional football for a long time and I've never seen a forward put away chances as clinically as Gray did in that match.'

As Robson added, 'Gray's aggression is almost stupefying. Our centre-backs were completely shattered when they came off the field at the end,' said the Ipswich manager. 'Gray never stopped challenging them, unsettling them. Every time they tried to get the ball away, Andy would be there to put pressure on them. They were happy to get into the bath, I can tell you.'

Brave as a lion – that's Andy Gray. But he has the ability, too, especially in the air. Andy, indeed estimates that 50 per cent of his goals come through headers.

Has he improved since he went to Villa?

'Yes,' he says. 'For the single reason that English football is more competitive than it is in Scotland. When I was with Dundee United some of the matches were pretty easy. But, to be honest, I haven't found any easy matches at Villa. They've all been like cup finals. This has helped me a great deal in the sense that I've become sharper and more alert.

'I anticipate things much more quickly now. I seem to have speed of thought as well as speed of movement now.

'But I'm lucky to be playing for Villa, for they believe in attacking football.'

Gray is a natural. And not surprised that the Drumchapel boy has made such an impact in England is his former manager, Jim McLean of Dundee United, who says:

'Frankly, Andy is no better now than he was at Tannadice. I'm delighted for him. He deserves all the success he can get. We really didn't do a great deal for him at Tannadice. He already had it all when he came here at the age of sixteen. All we did was polish it up. Andy has it all, plus the spirit to fight for a 50–50 ball.'

Too much of a fighter? Not really. Although he was sent off in the World Cup with the Czechs in Prague, he was sorely provoked and retaliated. But, as he said later, 'That taught me a bitter lesson. I'll know better next time. Actually, I should have known better in Prague. But I was kicked and punched and elbowed in the face by Czech defender Ondrus, and I hit back. It's all part of experience and of learning. You've just got to keep your head when you're playing.'

United received a fee in excess of £110000 from Villa, plus a number of clauses in the contract which would increase the money if he did certain things. Now Andy is the one striker in Britain in the £400000 bracket.

Gray, however, is paying the penalty for bravery and bears the marks most strikers retain as permanent decorations in the warfare of football in the seventies.

For weeks he spent four hours every day on the treatment table and two days before a match he suffered painful injections. These were desperate efforts by his club to have him fit, which shows how valuable Villa reckon he is.

His vibrant, tearaway style makes him

Andy Gray was twenty-one when this picture was taken – which is a blow to defenders. For the young Scot has years and years yet in which to put defences under his own particular brand of pressure.

the victim of hard tackles. But Andy considers a long rest will cure his thigh injury, the hoodoo of so many great players, including Eddie Gray of Leeds United.

Andy played all around Drumchapel as a schoolboy and a juvenile. 'I always wanted to be a professional footballer,' he said. 'I took eight O-levels at school but I never thought of going to university. I just wanted to play football.'

No one's more modest than the likeable Andy, who says: 'I'm by no means the perfect striker. What I lack is really good ball control and a good right foot. But I'm working on these. At Villa we put great emphasis on improving ball control, passing and shooting and going back to basics.

'Why not? Look at that star golfer Jack Nicklaus. He has never lost sight of the need to keep working hard on the fundamentals of the game and before the start of each season he goes back to his old teacher to polish his basic technique. We should do the same in football. It's paying off for Aston Villa.'

Andy, twenty-one last season, considers that while a person who has the basics can build other skills around them, goal-scoring ability is something else.

'Goal-scorers are born, not made,' he believes. 'Some players have tried dreadfully hard to become strikers and have failed to knock it off. I think I was born to score goals.'

Has Andy any secrets for aspiring strikers? 'Sorry, no,' he smiles. 'As I say, strikers are born. For instance, automatically good strikers get into scoring positions and half the time they wonder how they got there.'

Andy leads a happy and busy life in Birmingham. He has his own house in a garden suburb, is a co-director of a hairdressing business and is involved in advertising.

He is a level-headed young man and still blinks when he considers his startling rise to fame.

Playing for Clydebank Strollers at fifteen . . . on the Tannadice ground staff a year later . . . three matches with the Dundee United reserves . . . into the first team and instant success . . . transferred to Villa at nineteen in 1975 . . . now he is kingpin of a famous Aston Villa attack.

The Villa crowd love him. Andy, a trier, brought them hope when he was signed and backed that with great goals.

Many people in Scotland hope that it won't be long until Andy teams up with Willie Pettigrew of Motherwell in the international team. They believe this would be a partnership to bring glory to Hampden again. These two weren't all that impressive when they played together in an Under-23 team in a friendly against Leeds United but it takes time for such a partnership to operate effectively.

Both were inclined to go for the same balls, but both have matured since then, and both would love to play together in the same Scotland team.

And most of us who love exciting, attacking football that brings goals would love to see them there.

WHY ANDY HAD TO GO
by Jim McLean

How do you tell a seven-year-old boy that he won't see his favourite soccer star in action again at his favourite ground?

Breaking that sort of bad news to a football-crazy youngster is difficult for anyone, any time. But when you have to go home and tell your own son that you have just sold the player in question it is many times worse, believe me.

This is exactly what happened to me one night in 1975 when I drove from Tannadice to my home in Broughty Ferry to confront my son Gary with the news that the club had just sold Andy Gray to Aston Villa.

Andy didn't have a bigger fan than my young lad, who had even insisted that my wife should sew a big No. 10 – just like the one Andy wore in our side – on the back of his tiny Dundee United shirt.

So when I broke the news to Gary that night and saw his tearful reaction I knew exactly how the fans of the club, both young and old, would feel about the news.

I can tell them now that I was as upset as any of the supporters that United had been forced to let Gray go south. But big money transfers have always been part and parcel of the game in Scotland.

Let me say now that Dundee United have taken a lot more than the £110000 figure which was quoted at the time of Andy's move. That was merely a starting figure and the various clauses written into the deal have since produced quite a bit extra.

However, whatever the final transfer figure happened to be, the move was neces-sary at that particular stage. We have always struggled to attract big crowds at Tanna-dice, no matter how well we are doing or how many fine young players we produce.

And that season we had just spent over £20000 to bring our floodlighting system up to the standards demanded by UEFA for TV broadcasts. No Scottish provincial club can face bills like that without giving serious consideration to a big-money offer from England for one of their players.

But this is not an article about the finan-cial problems of Scottish football. It is a tribute to Andy Gray and let me say right away that my lad Gary and thousands of other young football fans throughout Britain could not possibly have a better hero.

Andy is an exceptional footballer as well as an exceptional character, a rare combina-tion that makes a manager's job more satis-fying and a little bit easier.

I first saw him playing in a closed doors game at Tannadice when he was just fifteen. He scored a goal that night, took up great position and we had him on an S form just as soon as the match was over.

Maurice Friel, the scout who had first spotted Andy playing in a public park in Clydebank, and I were totally convinced that we had signed a player who was bound to make it all the way to the top.

That view was strengthened even before he eventually joined us as a full-time player

Manager Jim McLean of Dundee United

Andy Gray in action

at the age of seventeen. We kept an eye on his progress and, in every grade he tackled at club or international level, he continued to get rave notices by scoring magnificent goals.

And so it was when he made his United debut against East Fife in the League Cup only a few weeks after coming to Tannadice as a full-timer. He got one of the goals in our 5–2 victory with the typical header.

Of course, he has never looked back, quickly making every new challenge a new success.

And he deserves all the success in the world and I am not about to take any of the credit for that, simply because Andy is a natural. All I did for the player was get him fit. The rest fell naturally into place through his great ability in the air, his instinctive positional sense and his dangerous left foot.

We did work on him but found that his class shone through even in these special sessions. When we worked with Andy we had to give him really difficult things to do. With other players we used to give them good crosses from the wings to improve their finishing. With Andy, we had to put in intentionally bad crosses to really stretch his ability. And, as often as not, he would stick the ball away.

Along with these obvious attributes, Andy Gray also has courage on his side. He simply does not see defenders' boots or goalkeepers' fists when he goes for the ball in the area. He is oblivious to everything but the ball and the goal.

Again this is natural. He proved that regularly to me by putting as much effort into getting to balls in practice matches as he would in serious games. Often there was a chance that he would injure himself or other players in these practice matches but no one could tell him to cut it out.

There have been suggestions down south that Andy will lose that aggression when he sustains one serious injury. English defenders who think they are in for an easier time from Andy once that happens – and, touch wood, it won't – had better forget it. Nothing will change his will to win.

I saw that very early in his career at Tannadice when he required a cartilage operation. Just four weeks and three days later he came back for a cup-tie at Dunfermline and might have had a hat-trick in the first 15 minutes. The injury and operation had killed none of his determination to be there first and have a go at the half-chance.

These examples give you an idea of Andy Gray the player. I am proud to have worked with him . . . and just as happy to have known him as a person. For, off the field,

Andy sets an example to every youngster in the game. I can best sum it up with a couple of little stories about him.

When he came to sign before his second season – by then he was already established – he was quite prepared to put pen to paper on a blank contract.

The club had treated him well in the past and he was content to accept that they would continue to do so without seeing the terms in black and white, even though he knew by then, as I did, that he was about to become one of the hottest properties in British football.

And no matter how much publicity or how many big money deals he may become involved in, Andy will never forget his beginnings in the game or that football provides his living. I have a letter in my possession thanking me and everyone else at Tannadice for their help. Andy, it was a pleasure.

Just as it is a pleasure to keep watching his progress in England. It takes quite a bit for me to think of anything other than my own team's performance at 4.45 on a Saturday afternoon. But when I do get round to finding out what is happening in the rest of the football world, my first question is: 'How did Aston Villa do?' And the second: 'Did Andy Gray get a goal?'

And if the answers come back 'They won' and 'Yes', everyone at Dundee United is a little bit happier.

This is the picture which shows just how torrid Scottish soccer is. It's action, action all the way, determination to get to the ball first, to put it into the net or clear the lines, as Celtic attackers and Airdrie defenders go all out.

RED HOT ACTION...
That's what the Fans really want

You'll never stop this argument. Should Scotland revert to the old-time football, that game of magical moves, beautiful ball control, sleek, silken passes, oily swerves, slow, often elaborate moves – the football, indeed, that is played today in so many parts of Europe?

Or would our followers of football yawn, and demand the style that is favoured today – the football that is played at hurricane pace, involves tackles to make you wince,

calls for strength and speed above all, and brings red-hot action?

ACTION – that's what the average fan wants. And can you really blame him? We need excitement nowadays in our lives.

And, thank goodness, despite all the complaints about our game, Scottish soccer still provides he-man battles, thrilling moves, great goals.

Here are dramatic pictures of incidents which had the crowds gasping:

Left: Even the referees have to be tough in football. Here referee John Paterson of Bothwell takes a bump as St Mirren try to score against Falkirk.

Below left: Determination – it's written all over the face of Hearts' powerful Drew Busby as he beats Motherwell's Gregor Stevens in a tackle and strides manfully on.

Below: Another sparkling winger who combines trickery with pace is Paul Wilson of Celtic, finding a way through a wall of Ayr United defenders at Somerset Park.

Right: Power is needed to make our Scottish soccer exciting. But there are still players who ally great skill to pace and strength. One is that dapper Hearts winger Rab Prentice, in action here against Dumbarton.

Oooooh! No wonder the big crowd at Ibrox sighed. They thought it was a goal all the way for Rangers – until Cammy Frazer of Hearts saved the day for his team with a cute overhead saving kick.

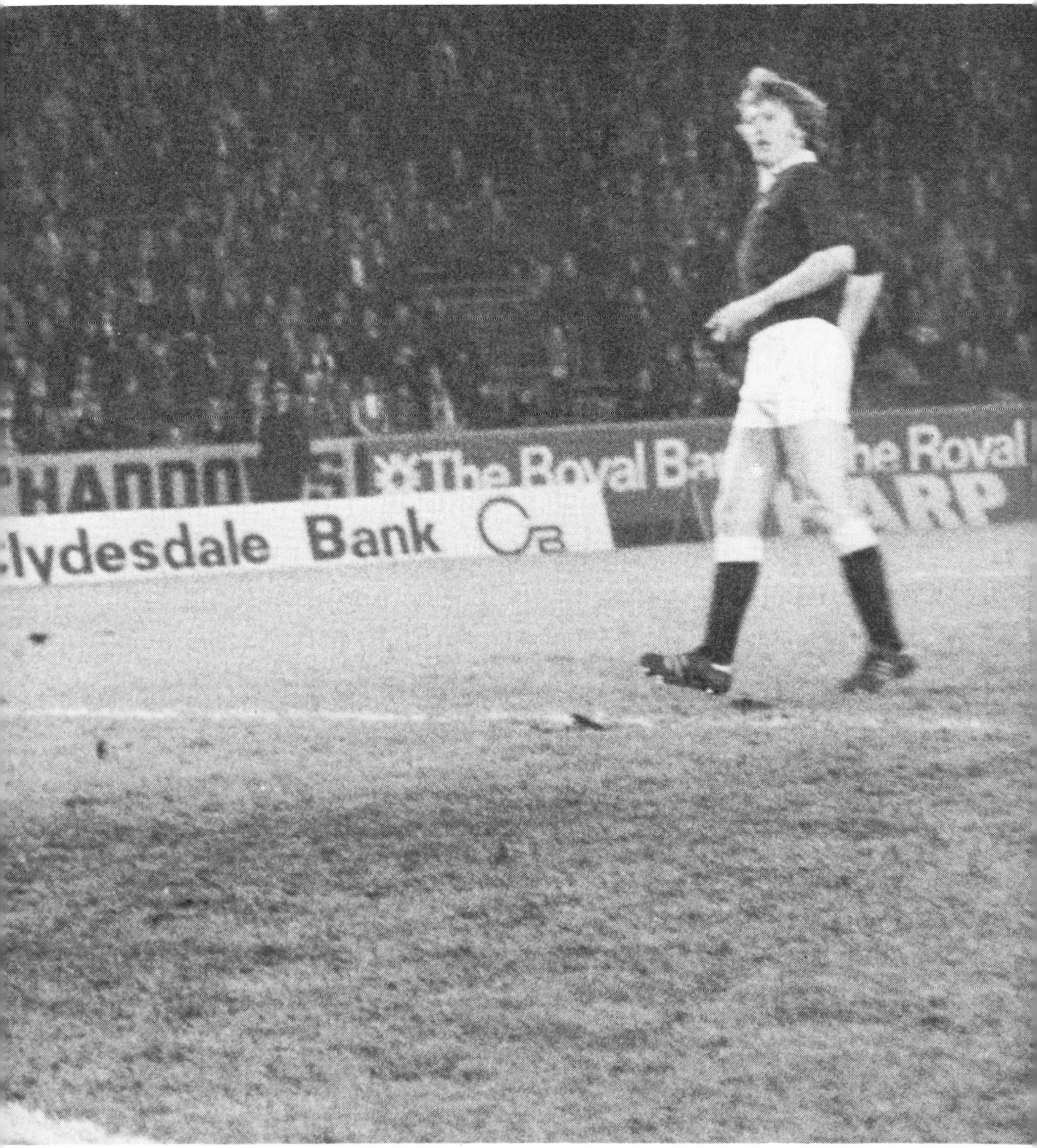

Clydesdale Bank
The Royal

Super saves still bring the fans to their feet, and Mike MacDonald of Hibs earns the cheers for this magnificent effort in a match against Celtic.

Hair-raising — sometimes that's Scottish soccer. But Kilmarnock's tall Derrick McDicken hasn't a thought for his hair style as he rises to head for goal in a game against Rangers at Ibrox.

Bravest man in a football team? The goalkeeper, of course. He's just got to be nowadays; just like Airdrie's Marshall Poulton — as he proves in making a gallant save in a fierce Clydebank raid.

This is the dashing attacker our crowds love — Derek Johnstone of Rangers going in hard to try to score against Ayr United.

THE HARSH WORLD OF THE REFEREE

The real reason referees are unpopular in football is that we look on them as schoolmasters – and exceedingly dour, grim schoolmasters at that. We do not regard them as complete neutrals, on the field to control the game, to see that the rules are obeyed, to make sure there is no nonsense. Not at all. We see in the referee the man who is taking his spite out on our team, who is in the pay of our opponents, who is in dire need of spectacles. Most of all, we see in the referee the frowning dominie of our youth, the teacher always reaching for his tawse, the sour authority who ensures that everything is done by law, the ancient who allows no frivolity or pranks. And all that is unfair to referees, an unassuming body of men without whom, don't let's forget, there would be no football.

Of course, we are apt to say that the referee wants too much of the limelight nowadays, fails to play to the advantage rule just so that he can wave his arms histrionically, blow his whistle fiercely and become the centre of attraction.

But we don't realize just how much the referee has to know, what pressures he works under, how dedicated he is. Certainly a referee must be dedicated for who wants to hear himself described week after week as a nutter, a robber, an idiot, a clown, an ass, a buffoon?

A referee must have a sense of humour. After all, who was responsible for the most famous passage ever written about a referee, which went like this:

'Of all the blear-eyed nincompoops that ever appeared in spindle-shanks on the turf in the guise of a referee, that cachinnatory cough-drop who attempted the job on Saturday was the worst we have ever seen. His asinine imbecility was only equalled by his mountebank costume and his general appearance and get-up reminded one more of a baked frog than a man. No worse tub-jumping, pot-bellied, jerry-built jackass ever tried to perform as a referee.

'His lugubrious tenebrousness and his monotonous squeaking on the whistle were a trial to the soul. Encased in a dull psychological envelopment of weird chaotic misunderstandings of the rules, he gyrated in a ludicrously painful manner up and down the field, and his addle-headed, flat-chested, splay-footed, cross-eyed, unkempt, unshaven, bow-legged, humpbacked, lop-eared, scraggy, imbecile and idiotic decision when he ruled Jones's second goal off-side, filled the audience, players and spectators alike, with disgust.'

Responsible was one, William Pickford, a well-known referee of the past, who wrote 'The Referee's Chart of 1893' on which all modern practice is founded.

Referees have a long and honourable past. They were first mentioned in soccer played at Cheltenham College away back in 1867. Before that, the practice in most important matches was to appoint two umpires, one from each side. At Cheltenham, though, it was decided that 'in every important match there shall be an umpire for each side (each captain to choose his own) and a referee, to be chosen by these umpires. Any point on which the umpires cannot agree shall be decided by the referee.'

Next, the English Association appointed in 1871 a referee for cup finals. And so eventually it was a case of one referee for one match.

Increased competition was the reason for the appointment of referees. The attitude of the players was changing and the days of the gentlemen players, proud of the manner in which rival teams generally conducted themselves and settled any disputes were beginning to fade. The time had come not only to specify the appointment of both umpires and the referees but to insist on all being neutral.

It wasn't until 1891 that umpires were abolished in favour of linesmen when the referee was moved from the touchline on to the field of play and empowered to give decisions without waiting for appeals to the umpires.

So the referee was in complete control and the demand for his services increased so quickly that in 1893 the first Referees' Association was formed.

Incidentally, the first fees for referees, fixed in 1888, were 10s 6d for the main officials and 5s for the linesmen.

Not everyone in the game, however, considered that a referee was needed. And there was conflict. For instance, that great Scot, Lord Kinnaird, a notable player, felt the introduction of a referee would make the game namby-pamby. But Sir Francis Marindin, one of the first referees who was to become President of the FA, considered the days of hacking were over.

No one was better known for use of the boot – in the wrong place – than Lord Kinnaird, star of the famous Wanderers, who played in nine English cup finals, wore long white trousers and a cricket cap and boasted a blazing red beard – a fearsome figure on the field of play.

It was Sir Francis Marindin who first made the remark that has been attributed to more modern participants of football – the response to Kinnaird's mother, who said to Marindin one day that she feared dear Arthur would return from that horrid, rough football with a broken leg and was told drily: 'Never fear, madam, it won't be his own.'

But Kinnaird is famous for saying, when asked by a rival captain 'Shall we play fair or shall we have hacking?' those immortal words: 'Oh, let's have hacking by all means.'

No wonder the game needed referees. Just read these notes of a session of the Football Association made away back in the days when disagreement arose about how the game should be played. . . .

'The secretary of the FA (Mr Morley): I think that the hacking is more dreadful in name and on paper than in reality. But I object to it most because I think that its being disallowed will promote the game of football and if we have hacking then no one who has arrived at the years of discretion will play at football and it will be entirely relinquished to schoolboys.

'A member of the FA (Mr Campbell): I approve now of the laws proposed against hacking to be expunged. I am afraid that there are many of the clubs who will not join the Association because they fear that our rules will do away with the skill shown in the game at Harrow and Eton and the

This referee isn't too popular with Celtic skipper Kenny Dalglish, is he? The reason? A spot of controversy over a penalty kick awarded to Dundee United.

pluck so necessary in the game as played at Rugby. Hacking is the true football game and if you look into the Winchester records you will find that in former years men were so wounded that two of them were actually carried off the field. Lately, however, the game has become more civilized than that state of things which certainly was, to a certain extent, brutal.

'People object to hacking because too many of the members of clubs began late in life and were too old for the spirit of the game. If you do away with hacking you will do away with all the courage and pluck of the game and I will be bound to bring over a lot of Frenchmen who could beat you with a week's practice. We all like the running and the hacking and will not play any other game.'

This was, then, the crucial time for referees. The 1880s marked one of the greatest transitional periods in the history of football.

Before the decade was over, the traditional 'gentlemanly' but far tougher football of the ex-public schoolboys was to disappear from the playing fields to be superseded by the subtleties and skills of the professional performers who valued their limbs as stock-in-trade and achieved their effects by cunning rather than by the unquestioning zeal of those who modelled themselves on the Light Brigade.

The referee had to be awarded fresh powers in the control of the game. He was empowered, for example, to keep time, to caution those who displayed ungentlemanly conduct and order them off if they persisted in their transgressions. It was the end of the Old Boy supremacy and the advent of professionalism. It was the era of the referee.

But, of course, criticism of referees has never really stopped.

Young men, nevertheless, still want to be referees. One of the most important aspects is knowing the laws of the game. Here are a few tips from an expert to youngsters who fancy themselves as the new Peter Craigmyle or Bobby Davidson.

Don't forget that the laws of the game are intended to provide that games should be played with as little interference as possible and it is the duty of the referee to penalize only deliberate breaches of the law. Constant whistling for trifling and doubtful breaches produces bad feeling and loss of temper on the part of the players and spoils the pleasure of spectators.

You can say that again, sir. Referees must use their heads.

How can referees win the respect of players and spectators? They must learn and understand every law, must be absolutely fair and impartial in every decision, keep physically fit and in good training.

Officials must understand – and so should fans – that the ball is out of play if, while in the air, it goes over the touchline even if it lands in the field . . .

That it is jumping at an opponent, and not jumping at the ball, that is a foul . . .

That unless the hand or arm strikes or propels the ball it is not a foul – far too often a player is penalized when the ball touches his arm through no intentional action of his own . . .

That it is not necessary to wait until the ball is out of play or for a stoppage in the game before giving a signal to a player that he may join or rejoin his team . . .

That when awarding an indirect free-kick the decision should be indicated by raising one arm above the head . . .

There's much more to being a good referee than knowing all the laws.

The good referee must remember that he can't please all the people all the time. Indeed, it's impossible for the greatest referee in the world to please a fraction of the fans at any time.

A budding referee must make up his mind early on in his career that not only must he be *au fait* with all the laws, he must explore the main purpose behind each one, its application and effect. If he does, he will discover that each law is based on commonsense and fairness. The matter of using good judgement in applying them when making decisions will give a person the courage of his convictions when officiating at the game.

Knowledge, real knowledge, of the rules will help referees to get along and please instead of irritating everyone. Getting along with people is one thing, pleasing them is another. A quick and correct decision will draw the respect of the public, even if the decision pleases only some of them. Half-hearted decisions please no one.

Anyhow, while the poor old ref may be the friend of few, he can always say that he is qualified by examination – and a pretty stiff examination at that – to do his job.

Which is more than most spectators are, never mind MPs and bailies. . . .

TV—My Lucky Mascot
by John Fletcher, Arbroath

The moment I walked into Gayfield on 12 March 1977, I felt sure that Arbroath were on the way to their first ever Scottish Cup semi-final.

For there, on the far side of the ground that would soon be crammed with an all-ticket crowd for our tie against local rivals Dundee, were my lucky mascots – the television cameras.

Arbroath are not what you would call one of soccer's most fashionable outfits and in all my time at Gayfield, I had appeared only twice in televised games prior to that quarter-final against Dundee.

Yet I had very good cause to remember the previous two occasions in which the cameras had turned up at our games.

The first had been at Ibrox three years earlier in a league match against Rangers. And I scored two of the goals that gave Arbroath a surprise win by 3–2 . . . the first time the club had beaten Rangers anywhere or in any competition.

But I have an even better memory of my second appearance on the box. That was on 2 March 1977, when we faced Hibs at Easter Road in a fourth round replay in the Cup.

Frankly, I shall always believe that the television cameras should not have been at Easter Road that night.

We had met Hibs at Gayfield on the previous Saturday and we should have

John Fletcher of Arbroath

knocked them out there and then. Tommy Yule put us in front early in the second half and it took a goal by defender John Blackley to earn them a replay.

We had chances to score more goals but it was obvious that not many bookmakers saw the first game because they made us 8–1 against in the replay.

That didn't worry any of the Arbroath players for, having played really well against them on one occasion, we felt we had nothing to fear in the second meeting.

And the fact that the TV cameras were at Easter Road for the game didn't do my confidence any harm.

However, there was a set-back after only 5 minutes of the replay. Gordon Marshall, our veteran goalkeeper, got into a muddle when the ball came over from the left and Ally McLeod was able to give Hibs the lead.

For a spell after that very little went right for us . . . except that Hibs could not add to the lead from the chances they made. Gradually, however, we began to play with a bit of confidence and Hibs appeared to lose some of theirs as their supporters became restless. Then, suddenly, we came up with something that made the Easter Road fans somewhat more than restless.

We equalized in 64 minutes when Tommy Yule picked up a poor clearance, moved in on goal, and had a shot deflected into the net.

And soon there was my magic moment in front of the TV cameras. Tommy broke on the left again and cut the ball back into the middle, where one of our players and a defender missed it.

The ball ran towards me, and, thinking back on it now, I probably should have set it up for Pat Gardner who was coming in fast just beside me.

It wasn't really on for a shot but I managed to curl my foot around and make a good contact. I suppose it could have hit the corner flag but, instead, it flew past Mike McDonald into the net. 2–1 Arbroath.

Hibs made more chances to equalize but they couldn't and, while many people thought we were lucky winners, I can only repeat that the replay should not have been necessary.

The happy memories of that game didn't end with the final whistle. It was hurriedly arranged that the Arbroath party should return to the hotel in Edinburgh where we had taken our pre-match meal to watch highlights of the game on television – and didn't it look good over a celebration pint!

And next morning there was another scene I won't forget in a long time, when I walked into the school in Montrose where I work as a Physical Education teacher. For even though most of the youngsters support Montrose, the traditional local rivals of Arbroath, I was given a rousing welcome. All that mattered to them was the fact that they had a TV 'star' in their midst.

So you can appreciate that the appearance of the television cameras for the quarter-final against Dundee – incidentally, it was the first time they had ever visited Gayfield – gave my own confidence a little extra boost.

And, after only a minute of the game, we looked good for a place in the semi-finals. Skipper Jimmy Bone sent Tommy Yule clear on the left and he put us a goal in front.

Dundee worked hard for an equalizer and, before half-time, they pulled us back with a goal from Gordon Strachan.

It remained anyone's game until luck deserted us in the last eight minutes of play. Just when everything pointed to another replay, we went up the field and a Jimmy Bone cross got through to Tommy Yule just a few yards out.

Tommy, who had scored three important goals against Hibs and Dundee, hit it just right but somehow the ball came back off the post with Ally Donaldson helpless.

It was a bad blow, but worse was to come. With three minutes left Dundee, who had seemed happy at the prospect of another chance, went upfield and Eric Sinclair scored with a header. Then, just one minute later, he scored again to make it 3–1 at the finish.

It was a shattering experience and I think even the Dundee fans in the crowd felt a little bit sorry for the way we had gone out.

However, the cup run did achieve one thing for the club. Manager Albert Henderson, who had offered his resignation earlier in the season when things were going really badly, was rewarded with a new contract. That was some consolation for all of us.

WHAT'S IT ALL ABOUT THEN?

Like every other season, 1976–7 had its moments of drama, excitement, fear, horror and fun. Like every other, too, it had its perplexing moments – moments which afterwards had us all muttering, 'Now then, what was that all about?'

Moments like these:

It looks like a picture from snow frolics at St Moritz. Actually, it's from Firhill, that famous ground where practically everything happens. Who's the mystery man, sprawling in the snow like a bobsleigh competitor hurled out at a bend? He's John Blackley of Hibs, and, avoiding the tackle, is Partick Thistle's George Mackie. They're certainly a hardy lot, Scottish footballers, to turn out in conditions like these.

Left: What's he looking at — and how did he rise so high above the rest? In fact Ally Scott of Hibs is cursing his luck. He put in a superb header in a game against Celtic — only to see the ball bounce off the bar.

Below: Now then, who's holding who? Arm-in-arm together at Rugby Park are Kilmarnock's Billy Murdoch and Celtic's Roddy McDonald.

Right: Oh dear, where did that one go? Clydebank players anxiously watch from their wall as a free kick taken by Dundee's Strachan flies narrowly past.

Left: Let me go, please release me! That seems to be the plea of Ayr United's Dixie Ingram as Celtic keeper Peter Latchford gets a hand into the affair.

Below left: Come on, ref, play the game. It was a goal! Celtic's Ken Dalglish shows his anger as a goal against Kilmarnock is ruled out because the referee considered the player was offside.

Right: Just look who's here! Fans in the stand at Kilmarnock's Rugby Park clamour for autographs as members of the Scotland squad, who had been training at the Ayrshire coast for the international against Wales, make their way to their seats to watch a game with Rangers. Can you spot the stars? Among them are Jim Brown, Hearts, Bobby Clark, Aberdeen, Ken Burns, Birmingham, Gordon McQueen and Eddie Gray of Leeds United.

Below: Looks like a shoemakers' nightmare, doesn't it? Boots, boots, boots — but which are the right pair? That's important when the pitch looks treacherous. So Celtic try various types before taking the field at Parkhead for a match with Ayr United. Danny McGrain reckons training shoes are the best bet.

Left: Hullo, hullo, what's going on? It's not one of football's most enjoyable moments. As Motherwell and Rangers players leave the field after a tough tussle at Fir Park, there's a flare-up on the way to the tunnel. Keep your heads, lads.

Below: No, this isn't as bad as it looks — not a punch-up or a knock-out. Just a moment of despair for Ayr United's goalkeeper Andy Geoghan and little Gordon Cramond after they tried to stop Kenny Dalglish of Celtic from scoring — in vain.

Right: Hey, get off my back. And Ayr's John Murphy doesn't like it a bit when Celtic's Joe Craig appears to be playing leapfrog.

WHEN IT'S TIME FOR A LAUGH IN FOOTBALL– the Fans read Sportsbag

Football fans often shout at the referee, pour scorn on the players, battle with opposing supporters. They relish drama and excitement. But there's nothing the Scottish fan loves more than a laugh.

And that's why the famous Sportsbag column in the Daily Record *is the most popular of them all. It's the column in which readers really have their say – as Hugh Taylor knows only too well! For Sportsbag is conducted by Scotland's best-known sports journalist and author. And it's quite a job.*

Sportsbag letter-writers pull no punches, tell the world just what they think about the game – and especially what they think about Taylor, accused of being everything from a Blue-nose to the World's No. 1 Idiot. Taylor, though, is no sitting duck. He hits back just as hard – and the fans love it all . . . which is why so many take the time and trouble to write to him.

Sportsbag – smiling, grave, authoritative, ferocious, humorous, angry, original – is the most entertaining column in Scottish sport, thanks to the readers. It may sometimes be daft, completely out of order. But it's never dull – as you can see by these examples from Sportsbag columns, which invariably bring a grin to an often grey world of sport . . .

Letters pour into Sportsbag every week and that gives Hugh Taylor, obviously reading a really funny one here, his toughest task of the week – selecting from the huge pile the letters he considers the best.

A new angle on football hooliganism from R. Leslie of Methil, who writes:

'Mr Taylor, you are right when you say the only punishment for soccer thugs should be a lengthy term of imprisonment. I cannot understand magistrates who let offenders off with a small fine.

'I would go further, however, and take a tip from the Scandinavian countries who make culprits work on the roads. Hard labour is what those people who disgrace football need most.'

* *I'm with you. And I'd make the hooligans work on the Road to Siberia!*

When Hugh Taylor reported a women's football match at Greenock one Saturday he gave Sportsbag readers one of the happiest days of their lives. How they sniped. . . .

'I see you've found your proper place at last. You write like a big lassie, so it's only right that you should go and report a big lassies' game.' – T. McKellar, Portobello.

'Do us another favour. Stop reporting the real matches and continue to go to the girls' games. It's more your style, dear.' – T. Rankin, Kilmarnock.

'You'll be saying next that Scotland can win the World Cup with a team of girls.' – H. McGill, Stranraer.

* *Well, we still haven't won it with a team of men, have we?*

Sample of the high regard in which Taylor is held by his readers is shown in this letter which came from R. Lawson, Aberdeen: 'Will you never learn sense? You and some of your more ignorant readers may think it's funny when you talk about your allegiance to Celtic and Rangers.

'I think it's dreadful. You do a lot of harm with your pandering to the big two. It's reporters like you who hurt the so-called provincial clubs.

'You can protest all you want to but the truth is that you don't really like any clubs except Rangers and Celtic. If you spent more time and space on my team Aberdeen, Dundee United, Hibs, Partick Thistle, Kilmarnock and the rest, you would foster football. Instead, we get nothing but headlines about the Old Firm.

'You may imagine you're a wee comic with your cracks about your green eyes and ears and blue nose. Let me tell you, to everyone else it's a complete bore.'

* *Think so? Picasso didn't. I'm the only model he ever could paint true to life.*

And R. Bell of Leith had this to say: 'Scotland still produces the best players and I blame you people on the press for giving a wrong impression of the game in this country.

'You're a spiteful lot, always looking on the gloomy side.

'I bet you never earned a cheer for your actions in football.'

* *You're wrong, mate. Nobody ever got a bigger cheer in football than I did. It was the day I told my club I was packing it in.*

'Footballers should be like soldiers, neat and tidy on parade', wrote D. Armour, of Giffnock. 'They should set an example to the youngsters of today. After all, they are the modern idols.

'But too many are hairy twits. They should have a year in the Army. That would teach them. I don't see how anyone can play football with hair in his eyes. They'd play better and feel better if they were a little more tidy.'

* *You may have a point – but this reminds me of the story of the manager of a struggling Scottish club who was interviewing a young player. He told him severely: 'Look, lad, if you're going to join us, you'll have to get your hair cut. We don't like hippy types at our club.'*

Said the player: 'Ach, wait a minute, sir, it's the modern trend. Look at Georgie Best wi' his long hair.'

Said the manager sarcastically: 'And can you play like George Best?'

The player: 'Don't be daft. If I could play like Best, dae you think Ah'd want to join this lot o' yours?'

A complaint about too many women going to football matches came to Sportsbag from S. Jones of Bathgate. He wrote:

'Football is a man's game. We like to let off steam and we don't want women around when a game's on.

'Women's place is in the house. They don't understand football anyhow. Let them go to the pictures and Bingo – but keep them away from the fitba'.'

* *Which reminded Taylor of the Celtic supporter whose wife complained to him as he was off again to an away game. 'You swine, you think more of Celtic than you do of me.' To which he replied, 'Huh, I think more of Rangers than I do of you.'*

When David White was on the move from Ibrox a letter from D. McGrory of Stirling showed that the Big Two are the favourite subject for Sportsbag writers. Said reader McGrory:

'Rangers are the daftest club in the country. They should never have put the blame on manager White. Can't they see beyond their own noses?

'What they should have done is offered Celtic's Jock Stein £100000 tax free and a villa on the Riviera. No, not to become manager, but to quit the country.

'Jock is Rangers big trouble. If he hadn't been manager of Celtic, Rangers would still have been top of the heap in Scotland.'

* *Shows how little you know, son . . . Jock prefers a bungalow in Paradise.*

Sportsbag customers don't like referees very much. And refs at Old Firm games are always being criticized. Wrote P. Allan of Glasgow: 'It's high time a foreign referee controlled the Rangers–Celtic game. There is too much bitterness for a home official to have the responsibility.

'Even our top officials are criticized by the clubs. So let's go abroad for a man who will not be upset by the undercurrents and can't be blamed by either club for having bias.'

* *Hugh Taylor had the last word – and the last laugh. Bias at an Old Firm match? What about the Ne'erday game when two fans had been celebrating. At the interval, one said: 'Hey, Tam, hoo aboot giving the referee a wee dram oot o' your bottle?'*

'Not on your life,' said the other. 'He would come oot and see two teams in the second half.'

A PUBLIC SCHOOL FOR SOCCER–
George Young's Bright Idea

George Young, the former Rangers defender who was Scotland's greatest captain, last season came up with an idea which had every schoolboy in the land jumping for joy.

'Why not,' said George, 'have a real school for football in Scotland?'

Why not?

Some people will shudder and say: 'Don't be stupid. A school for football? Football's only a game, a side-issue in education. How dare this country pay money to train footballers?'

I'm not so sure. I agree with George Young. A school for young players isn't a far-fetched idea, and Young explains:

'Football is more than a game nowadays. It's a way of life. It's a rewarding career. Let's face it, it's more important to millions of people than politics, business or the arts. A victory by one nation over another at football is like winning a war. So don't let's turn up our noses and say a school for aspiring soccer stars is pie in the sky, a silly dream.

'Anyhow, sponsorship is in the football air just now with big business putting big money into the game. Wouldn't it be better for a firm to sponsor a school for kids instead of putting the money into the hat for top players and managers, who are pretty well paid?'

George Young when he was Scotland's most famous skipper.

If such a school were started George, who has done so much for the kids since he retired after a distinguished career as player and manager (with Third Lanark), feels there are plenty of sites in Scotland where the academy for football learning at its highest level could be built. One is the old Lanark Racecourse.

What would the school be like? There are several on the Continent, the most famous being at Appinano Gentile, a huge complex outside Milan in northern Italy.

Not only is that the training ground and hide-away for the AC and Inter-Milan clubs (and these players must stay there for four days at a time every week in the season), but it contains the most famous football boarding school in the world.

The best young footballers in the north of Italy get the chance of being educated in the school in the beautiful countryside. Soccer, of course, is high on the curriculum but some of the best teachers in Italy are on hand to ensure that the boys' education in all the other necessary subjects is of the highest order.

Other countries in Europe are now following the Italians. Not so long ago the new Karl Beck Sports School at Lindabrunn, in Austria, was opened.

This complex includes two playing pitches, running-track, hostel and lecture rooms. At the moment, short courses for everyone, from national team to schoolboy formations, are being held, but the Lower Austrian Football Association are considering starting long courses, combined with normal education, for pupils who are showing promise at soccer.

Perhaps the school that George Young dreams of will never be started in this country but other nations are leaving us behind in keeping alive the interest of children in football.

Listen to the thorough Konrad Dorner, assistant secretary of the West German FA, who said a short time ago: 'It is of primary importance for our football to pick up the threads of the great performances of our senior clubs. The basis for further development of our football can only be achieved by having a good crop of "future players".

'In this respect, even greater attention must be paid to technical and tactical training, and this starting with the children in the lowest age group. Each boy must be made fully aware that he can only improve his ability and proficiency through more and better individual training.

'Naturally, this means a heavier burden on the coaches and trainers in the clubs, coaching and community centres.'

And what did the Germans do after this?

Immediately after they had won the World Cup in 1974, they started this ambitious programme for youth: a youth league for the age group 14–15 in their eleven Proficiency Centres; a youth league for the age group 16–17, with matches being played on Sundays; and a big new competition for the league of players aged between 18 and 21 – a chance to play their matches as curtain-raisers to their First Division games.

That latter is a brilliant idea. It gives the lads their chance to become acclimatized to the big-time atmosphere.

Other European countries show, too, that George Young is merely talking sensibly when he calls for a school for footballers. Take Poland, whose national team's skilful play in the last World Cup was so widely admired.

More than 100000 youngsters play regularly there in organized competitions and the Polish FA attaches great importance to the instruction of the nation's youth. It spends a maximum of effort and money in providing the young players with optimal training conditions. There is an extensive match system as well as instruction courses for trainers and good training camps for the best young players.

Good training camps – that's the salient point. Another is the fact that in Poland young players get a chance to show their paces before big crowds with matches played before their seniors kick off. Would this take a trick in Scotland? Alas, most senior grounds are empty until just before the matches start – but pubs and betting shops are full!

I am told, however, that football is improving in Poland mainly because of their football schools, set up and run by many of the country's National League clubs. These include a normal school schedule but with time reserved every day for football.

Each of these special classes is run by one of the country's leading clubs. And it goes without saying that the best young players will eventually be taken under that club's wing.

If George Young's idea is ever taken up – and our dedicated coaches who do so much in Scotland without the best facilities are right behind him – he hopes, however, that our youngsters will not develop into robots.

'I don't believe in mass coaching,' he told me. 'How could you ever coach a natural – a Jimmy Mason, a Torry Gillick? What I want to see is the youngsters being taught the basics, the skills every player should master, and then being allowed to express themselves. I want a football school to ensure that the basic skills are properly taught.'

Certainly football has entered a new phase, with higher levels of physical train-

George Young, who now takes a great interest in schoolboy football, looks at some of the trophies he won in his distinguished career for Rangers and Scotland.

ing making the game faster and accelerating its rate of development.

After all, once football showed no changes for decades at a time. Look at how long it took for changes to be made in the offside rule, and the fact that it was then more than twenty years before the so-called WM-system had fully established itself as a counter-measure.

The Hungarians started a revolution with an original style. They didn't pass directly to a team-mate – they passed into the open space, then another player would suddenly make that space his own and move the ball on into another unmarked area.

Then Real Madrid and the Italians took over that system and developed it. Inter-Milan for instance, discovered how to mark forwards more closely and defenders moved like shadows as attackers went to collect the passes into no-man's-land. Inter started close man-to-man marking – but they also brought in a new element; they dropped back deep into their own half to start building up attacks from there.

But it must be remembered that innovations in football spring from talented individuals, primarily by instinct. And the Hungarians, Real and the rest were at their peak when they had magnificent individualists.

But what such players did so brilliantly can have the opposite effect when practised by less gifted players. And that was why these great teams faltered – they ran out of players of genius.

For it was all very well to drop back to your own penalty area when there was a Suarez or a Corso there to launch a Mazzola, Jair or Domenghini off on a new thrust forward. But when players simply fall back to cover their own goal and do not take the initiative themselves, while upfield there are only mediocre forwards lying in wait for passes, the crowd is not going to like it.

But changes today are adopted more quickly and the period of unattractive and disorganized play seems to be over.

In this new era, however, with players no longer specializing in one specific position but nearly all being able to tackle in defence as well as initiate and round off attacks, modern players have to possess all-round skills.

Certainly the game has become incomparably faster, more varied and more spectacular in many countries.

And if Scotland is to keep that blue flag flying high it seems to me that George Young's idea of a school for footballers must be adopted.

For players with flair must be given every chance to polish their skills.

HAIL! HAIL! THE CELTS ARE HERE AGAIN

It was a stroke of football genius that had all Scotland gasping. It was audacious, it was imaginative – and it was brilliantly successful. It could only have been executed by the greatest manager in the game – Jock Stein of Celtic.

It was the transfer of Pat Stanton from Hibernian to Parkhead.

Early in the season, Stein was worried. Back in charge of the club after a severe injury incurred in a car crash, Parkhead's big man was re-building a team to restore lost glory. To the fans, things were looking up. Bright youngsters such as Tommy Burns were making a hit.

Stein, master of all the soccer arts and crafts, knew better. He realized that he was asking too much of his up-and-coming players. The side needed experience and stability. It required a player of vast experience to bolster the defence and bring the best out of the lad carrying tremendous responsibility, Roddy McDonald, the tall Highlander who had assumed the awesome task of taking over from the King of Parkhead, skipper and centre-half Billy McNeill.

Stein thought about Pat Stanton. Although he was out of the picture at Easter Road, he had been the club's captain, had spent a long time there and it looked as though he was as permanently fixed in the capital as Edinburgh Castle.

But Stein got his man – and Celtic were on their way to a glorious season. They became again the best team in Scotland, winning the Premier League title and the Scottish Cup, and reaching the final of the League Cup.

Celtic's splendid players won the honours but it was the know-how, the inspiration of Jock Stein which really brought them back to the pinnacle, taking over from their old rivals, Rangers, who had gained supremacy the previous season.

Not only did Stein bring Pat Stanton to Parkhead, he perfected his pattern by buying Joe Craig from Partick Thistle and Alfie Conn, the former Rangers idol who had gone south to Spurs.

It was all part of the special magic that is Celtic, the Jock Stein magic. How do you analyse it? Certainly there is a potent compound in the spell over Parkhead. Perseverance is one ingredient. Stein is another – a dream manager. Versatility, resilience, imagination, pace, power – all these, too, play a part in Celtic's magical roundabout. My view is that Celtic are at the top because they never forget a rich heritage. They have more artistic, thinking players than most, Stein's formula for success doesn't change. Indeed, it is a continuation of the recipe which made the Celtic teams of the twenties and thirties so delightful to watch.

In those great old days, the heroes were the McGrorys, the Quinns, the Delaneys, the flamboyant, extrovert, dashing scorers who made the headlines. These stars, however, wouldn't have been lethal finishers without the aid of the men of genius, the astute wing-halves and inside-forwards of craft, cunning and superb control, among

'We've done it!' Celtic players show their joy after winning the League Championship.

them Patsy Gallagher, Alex Thomson, Malcolm MacDonald, Peter Wilson, elegant players whose skill set the Celtic pattern.

So it is today, Joe Craig fits into the Stein scheme perfectly, following strikers like Joe McBride, Willie Wallace and Dixie Deans; and making the play, are world class artists such as captain Kenny Dalglish, the peerless Danny McGrain and the skilful Alfie Conn, technically perfect in today's crisper soccer but nevertheless players who would have fitted in magnificently in the courtlier scene of yesteryear.

Stein has taken the gilt of the past and welded it to the chrome of modern soccer, embellishing it with that special magic of his own.

This is how Jock Stein sums up his football philosophy: 'I don't hide the source of my ideas. The great players who most influenced my thinking were Hidegkuti, Boszic, Kocsis, Lantos and Puskas – yes, the famous Hungarians. When I saw Hungary beat England in 1953 I knew this was to be the way football had to be played. Hungary had great individuals who could play as a team. There was no restriction on the players. They played where they wanted to, yet they were clever enough to play for each other.

Celtic captain Kenny Dalglish is carried aloft in triumph after the Premier League title has been won.

New 'Old Firm' favourites are Kenny Watson
of Rangers, and Alfie Conn, the former
Ranger who is now a Celtic star.

'So when I became manager of Celtic I
set about finding the same kind of players,
players who had a bit of flash about them,
who would encourage people to come and
watch them even if the team was having an
ordinary time. Players must have rapport
with the crowd – that's vital.'

Stein's latest double has given him
tremendous satisfaction – so much so that
he refused to leave the club to take over as
Scotland manager when Willie Ormond
resigned to join Hearts. It came two years

Another newcomer to Parkhead is former
Morton goalkeeper Roy Baines, seen here
clearing in a game with Dundee United.

after his history-making nine-in-a-row triumph and proves that he still has what it
takes to be the outstanding manager of his
time.

Because of his car accident he cannot
now don a track suit and take training as
he did before. He still misses the day-to-day
involvement but he is happy with the way
assistant manager, David McParland, takes
command at training and, of course, Stein
still has charge of the team and the selection.

Now Celtic are reaching another peak.
Stein says he wants one or two experienced
players to attain a pool strong enough to win
the European Cup again. But he is happy to
have a young, hungry team, eager for greater
success. Most of the Celts have years of football still in them. Failure and frustration –
they had been beaten in two League Cup

Finals and trailed in the previous season's championship and Scottish Cup – are behind them. The transitional spell is over. Celtic are well on their way again to becoming new Lisbon Lions.

Their greatest moment of the season came on 16 April 1977. That was when Celtic sprang back to an old familiar role by becoming the Premier League champions.

It was the first time they had taken the new title – but they had won the First Division 29 times. And what a day it was for the Celtic fans at Easter Road!

Angry Rangers players protest after referee Bob Valentine awarded a penalty to Celtic in the Scottish Cup Final.

The songs of Celtic jubilation might have been heard at Parkhead Cross, Glasgow. A rainbow of green and white blossomed all over the bleak terracings. There were 22000 spectators at the Hibernian–Celtic game – and 20000 of them must have been Celtic supporters.

This was how Celtic got the goal which brought them the title. . . .

Frustration was creeping in. Tension lined the faces of the Celtic players. Hibs were playing just as well as their opponents. It was hectic.

Suddenly Ronnie Glavin swept in. His shot had 'Goal' written all over it – until the ball hit the post.

Conn was there, however. A neat pass

across goal. And Joe Craig did it again. He couldn't miss that one.

Celtic had come a long way from October. A title seemed only a dream then. Celtic had taken only seven points from six games and it looked as though any of three other teams would make it a fierce competition for the top honour.

The turning point came for Celtic when they beat one of the best sides in the division, Dundee United, by 5–1.

From then on, they began to play in their old adventurous way. The other candidates failed. Celtic improved, and the league was theirs.

They completed the double with a 1–0 victory over Rangers in the Scottish Cup Final at Hampden on 7 May 1977.

The old ground was grey and rain-swept. A crowd of only 54 252 turned up, and, alas, the Final never became the classic we expected. Indeed, it was for Celtic a tactical triumph. Without the injured Ronnie Glavin, they changed their style. Marking was tight, with creative players like Dalglish, McLean, Alex MacDonald, Watson and Conn struggling to find space. And Icelander Shuggie Edvaldsson stuck so closely to Derek Johnstone throughout the entire game that the Ranger never got one chance of revealing his scoring prowess.

But if there was a lack of entertainment there was plenty of controversy. An incident in the 20th minute will be talked about as long as the Old Firm meet. . . .

At last the fouling stopped and it looked as though the Final was to explode into action. Goalkeeper Stewart Kennedy was injured when he collided with a post after stopping a header. Kennedy required treatment and, when the sponge was put away, Alfie Conn took a corner.

Up rose Celtic centre-half Roddy McDonald – to become the best player at Hampden – to meet the cross with his head.

And the match erupted.

The ball came back. Edvaldsson shot hard. On the line was Derek Johnstone. He stopped the ball. Was it with his hand? The referee had no doubt. He gave a penalty and refused to listen to violent Rangers protests.

When the row died down, up stepped Andy Lynch and the back coolly and competently blasted the ball past Kennedy to give Celtic the lead – and victory.

Afterwards, Rangers players said Johnstone had stopped the ball with his knee. Celtic attackers insisted a hand had been used. Slow-motion television pictures of the incident failed to clear up the mystery. But it didn't matter. Referee Bob Valentine was convinced it was a penalty – and his is the final decision.

Anyhow, the match improved in the second-half, and Celtic had the edge. They should have wrapped it up when Joe Craig, a yard offside, was allowed to go on and beat the onrushing Kennedy with his shot. But Joe sent the ball wide.

Near the end, Rangers brought on young Chris Robertson for Kenny Watson and three times the striker nearly saved the match for his team. One of his headers was brilliant – but the ball hit the bar with Peter Latchford helpless.

So Celtic won what was labelled the professional Final.

The teams were: Celtic – Latchford. McGrain, Stanton, McDonald, Edvaldsson, Lynch, Conn, Dalglish, Aitken, Craig, Wilson. Subs – Burns, Doyle.

Rangers – Kennedy, Jardine, Forsyth, Jackson, Greig, Hamilton, Watson, MacDonald, McLean, Parlane, Johnstone. Subs – Robertson, Miller.

Referee: R. B. Valentine, Dundee.

Football wasn't the victor at Hampden. Television was clearly the winner, for live coverage of the match on a dreary day resulted in the lowest Cup Final attendance since the war.

For the sake of an extra £12 000 fee for live coverage by television, the SFA – as Celtic insist – risk ruining the Cup Final as

Celtic centre-half Roddy McDonald was the man of the Cup Final. Here he clashes with Rangers' Colin Jackson and Tom Forsyth.

a spectator sport. The Celtic view is that there will be a disastrous attendance if the afternoon is miserable and neither Celtic nor Rangers are in the Final.

Before the sell out to sponsorship, some of the Cup Final crowds were: 1976 Rangers v Hearts 85 000; 1975 Celtic v Airdrie 75 000; 1974 Celtic v Dundee United 75 000; 1973 Celtic v Rangers 122 000; 1972 Hibernian v Celtic 106 102; 1971 Celtic v Rangers 120 000; replay 103 000.

These figures speak for themselves.